TOWARDS TRANSNATIONAL COMPETENCE

Rethinking International Education:

A U.S.-Japan Case Study

Prepared by The Task Force for Transnational Competence

A Project on Rethinking U.S.-Japan Educational Exchange
Sponsored by the United States-Japan Foundation and
Several Universities in the United States and Japan
and coordinated by SUNY Buffalo's
Center for Comparative and Global Studies

MAR 1998

Acknowledgments:

The Task Force wishes to express its special gratitude to the United States-Japan Foundation and to the following universities which generously supported the deliberations leading to this report: University of California, Los Angeles, SUNY at Buffalo, Boston College, Kokugakuin, Obirin, Tamagawa, Aichi Gakuen, and Nagoya University.

Institute of International Education
809 U.N. Plaza
New York, NY 10017

http://www.iie.org

ISBN: 087206-239-2

Table of Contents

TOWARDS TRANSNATIONAL COMPETENCE

Rethinking International Education

Executive Summary

The revolution in access to information, the end of the Cold War, and the success of the General Agreement on Trade and Tariffs (GATT) and other regional agreements in deregulating trade are contributing to the transformation of the role of the nation-state and a lowering of national boundaries. More salient in the years ahead will be those transnational political, economic, and personal networks that transcend traditional boundaries.

The task of future education will be to help individuals prepare for these new realities. Whereas education once focused on the values and skills necessary for strengthening nations, education in the future will need to place greater emphasis on **Transnational Competence** (TNC). Transnational Competence refers to the ability of individuals, organizations, communities, and governments to effectively cope with the rapidly changing transnational environment and to realize their goals. The core elements of TNC are:

Ability to imagine, analyze, and creatively address the potential of local economies/cultures

Knowledge of commercial/technical/cultural developments in a variety of locales

Awareness of key leaders (and ability to engage such leaders in useful dialogue)

Understanding of local customs and negotiating strategies

Facility in English and at least one other major language, and facility
with computers

Technical skills in business, law, public affairs, and/or technology,
and awareness of their different nature in different cultural contexts

In earlier eras, supra-local relations were structured either in international or multinational environments, which tended to be hierarchical in nature and often premised on a former colonial heritage. Elitist ties and power were the keys to success. Transnationalism refers to the emerging era where relations and networks are being formed around common interests, affinities, and sentiments, often with little regard for the constraints of conventional geographic space. Transnational Competence enables the formation and functioning of these networks.

This study, supported by the U.S.–Japan Foundation and universities in both countries, focuses on the examples of the United States and Japan, two of the dominant economies of the late 20th century. It explores the respective national experiences and particularly the efforts of these two nations to promote international education. It finds a striking asymmetry in these efforts, with the U.S. primarily oriented to Europe and Japan primarily oriented to the United States. Both nations place remarkably little emphasis on Asia even as that part of the world is becoming increasingly prominent in world affairs. Education in both nations needs to transcend these limitations.

This will be vital for:

Economic Survival: the most dynamic and balanced relations
between **corporations** are prevalent in those parts of the global
system where there is mutuality in Transnational Competence.

Political Stability: those local and national **governments** which share
the greatest depth and mutuality in Transnational Competence find it
easiest to solve old problems and evolve new relations.

Preservation of Human Dignity: those parts of the world whose
citizens excel in Transnational Competence are accorded the
greatest respect by the global community.

The report identifies six key areas requiring priority attention, especially in the United States and Japan:

1. Employers, as major beneficiaries (especially the information, communications, transportation, and finance sectors), should be asked both to stress the value of transnational learning experiences for employment and to provide financial support for these experiences.

2. Every high school and college youth should have the opportunity to engage in an intensive transnational learning experience for an extended period.

3. Transnational learning experiences should emerge from the commitment of local communities and institutions.

4. Major efforts need to be devoted to improving the quality and diversity of transnational learning experiences at all levels (high school, collegiate, professional/corporate, community) and to strengthening the related infrastructure.

5. It is essential to reinforce connections between the educational programs of different levels through sharing of personnel and other resources.

6. Sustained attention should be focused on improving the conditions for in-depth academic and scientific/technical cooperation between Japan and the United States, with special attention to expanding the flow of information and improving the accuracy of images.

The first two chapters outline the context for change, and the next three outline a framework for improvement and the rationale for reform in the United States and Japan. The final chapter reiterates the major recommendations and also identifies several areas for joint action. While the report focuses on the examples of the United States and Japan, it is believed that these have broader implications.[1]

Members of the Task Force on Transnational Competence

Yoshiya Abe is Professor of Comparative Religion at Kokugakuin University and a former administrator of two of the key Japanese government agencies involved in international education.

Philip Altbach is Professor at Boston College and Director of its Center for International Higher Education. Dr. Altbach is one of America's most astute and prolific chroniclers of the university in comparative perspective.

Peggy Blumenthal is Vice-President for Educational Services of the Institute of International Education, which administers USIA's Fulbright fellowship program and other exchanges and research activities.

---

[1] This report will also be published in Japanese, with some modifications to take account of the knowledge and priorities of the Japanese audience. A related volume which includes the various fact-finding and policy studies commissioned by the Task Force will be published next year, entitled *Rethinking International Education: Focus on the United States and Japan.*

William Cummings is Professor of Comparative Education at SUNY-Buffalo and a well-known observer of Japanese and Asian education; in 1990 with Gail Chambers he wrote *Profiting from Education* which examined the fate of overseas joint ventures in higher education. Several of his books have been translated into Japanese. He is the project leader for this grant from the United States-Japan Foundation, and coordinator of the Task Force.

John Hawkins is Dean of International Studies and Programs at UCLA and is currently a key player in the planning for Title VI legislation among America's leading universities.

Kasue Masuyama is a Lecturer in Japanese language at SUNY-Buffalo and is very active in developing programs to link university language education with the needs of schools and corporations.

Akimasa Mitsuta, a former Vice-President of the Japan Foundation and career official in Japan's Ministry of Education and Culture, is currently a Professor of Comparative Education at Obirin University.

Shigeru Nakayama, Japan's leading scholar on science history and the relation of science to society, is a Professor at Kanagawa University.

Samuel Shepherd is Executive Director of the U.S.-Japan Educational Commission in Tokyo, the binational agency which administers the Fulbright Program in Japan.

Yoshiro Tanaka is Professor of Education at Tamagawa University and one of Japan's most astute and prolific writers on international education.

Toru Umakoshi is Professor of Education at Nagoya University and Director of that university's new International Center. Dr. Umakoshi, who was formerly an official in the Ministry of Education and Culture, is one of Japan's best-known authorities on Korea.

Roberta Wollons is Professor of Japanese Studies at Indiana University-North and former Professor of American Studies at Doshisha University.

Richard Wood is Dean of the Yale Divinity School and former President of Earlham College, the U.S. college which sends the largest proportion of its students to Japan for study abroad. Dr. Wood is also Chairman of the U.S.-Japan Friendship Commission.

Introduction

Our goal in this report is to identify both a language and a strategy for improving U.S.-Japan "international education," with a special emphasis on issues of importance to Americans, where the challenges are greatest.

The policy review leading up to this report was carried out from 1994 to 1996 by a core group of international educators, primarily based in the United States and Japan. The first year was devoted to fact-finding, with six papers prepared by binational teams and presented to a larger group convened at the UCLA campus. In year two, several policy papers were commissioned to explore key issues in greater depth, and the main themes of these studies were debated on the campus of Kokugakuin University in Tokyo.[2] Year three has been devoted to the preparation of this volume, relying on several meetings of diverse groups of international educators to review recommendations and key concepts. The names of those attending these various events are listed in the appendix.

The group has focused on the U.S.-Japan exchange relationship, an enormously valuable and mutually enriching economic, political and cultural set of ties. Despite efforts on both sides to continuously improve this relationship, it still is characterized by significant imbalances in such areas as trade and information. Behind these imbalances is the simple fact that **Japan is one of those great exceptions to the proposition that English Is enough to get one by in the daily challenges of gathering information, negotiating contracts, and carrying out business**.

Japan is a complex society, and its people have deep reverence for their national language and culture. For Americans to do well in Japan, they need to have a trained facility in things Japanese. The acquisition of this facility cannot be obtained overnight. Indeed, one of the major conclusions of this policy review is that it is even difficult to develop sufficient facility within a collegiate or postcollegiate educational experience. Rather, the foundations are best built at an earlier stage. The propositions and recommendations that follow build on this fundamental conclusion. While Japan poses major challenges for inadequately prepared Americans, so do China, Russia, the Mideast, and elsewhere. Similarly, inadequately prepared Japanese encounter difficulties as they seek to build new transnational relations, especially in Asia, Africa, and Latin America.

Many of America's past efforts to strengthen competitiveness have been

---

[2] Most of the papers will be published in a parallel volume, *Rethinking International Education: Focus on the U.S. and Japan*, edited by Yoshiya Abe, William K. Cummings, John Hawkins, Kasue Masuyama and Yoshiro Tanaka.

quick fixes, model programs of a federal agency or foundation funded for a brief period of time and affecting a small, elite group. Such programs have little or no cumulative effect. We believe the challenge is great and requires a more systemic and comprehensive approach, involving all levels of our educational system and all sectors of our society. While the federal government has an important role to play in revitalizing international preparedness, in the future much more needs to be asked of our state and local governments, our grassroots organizations, and the businesses that choose to operate in the United States. Japan has been more systematic in preparing its citizens for interaction with the West, but woefully inattentive to the challenges posed by other transnational settings.

The fact-finding phase of this report reached several conclusions which are listed below and will be reviewed in greater depth in the first chapters of the report:

1. **International education can be stimulated by a new transnational rationale and greater involvement of nongovernmental actors**. The rationale we propose, to complement prevailing rationales, is the need to develop Transnational Competence.

Transnational Competence as embodied in individuals involves a combination of cultural and technical skills, and the foundations need to be established at an early age. Japan's school system is better designed for developing these foundations than is the American system. Especially troubling in the United States is the failure of more than two-thirds of America's school systems to require foreign languages and international studies.

2. **The current rationales for international education in Japan and the United States are divergent and lead to unnecessary misunderstandings.** The prevailing Japanese *ryugakusei* rationale stresses long-term commitment to gain knowledge and insight from a foreign expert. In contrast, the dominant American rationale of "mutual understanding" stresses moderate overseas exposure as a stimulus for expanding personal awareness. Thus the United States has been puzzled at why so many Japanese go overseas for so long, and Japan has, until recently, been unsympathetic to those young Americans who just want to stay in Japan for a few weeks or months. The difference in current ideologies is one reason for proposing a new and commonly shared ideology as a rationale for future programs. Transnational Competence is attractive to Japan, as it seeks to broaden its contacts, especially with Asia, and understands this approach as part of a multinational initiative. Similarly, Transnational Competence is attractive to the United States as it signals a new rationale for and level of purposefulness in international education.

3. **The long-standing American rationales of personal enrichment and mutual understanding dispose Americans to establish exchanges and look for balance**. Actually, America does not achieve balance with any nation, in virtually any category of international exchange—high school, collegiate, community, or corporate. But the imbalance with Japan is quite extreme, and the imbalance with other Asian countries such as China and Korea is also large. The differences are most easily illustrated with collegiate exchange data, though the pattern seems to hold no matter what level is considered.

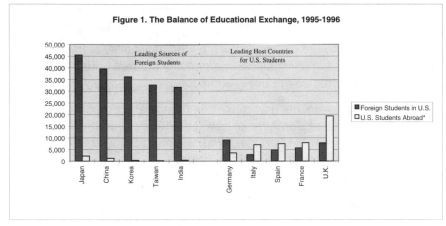

Figure 1. The Balance of Educational Exchange, 1995-1996

Source: *Open Doors 1995/1996: Report on International Educational Exchange, 1996. Todd M. Davis, ed., New York: I I E.*
*The data for U.S. students abroad is from 1994/1995

These disparities suggest it is time to drop the notion of reciprocity and "balance," and instead ask, **What level of Japan-related Transnational Competence is "sufficient" for the United States** at any given time? How can that be developed? With over 45,000 Japanese studying in U.S. universities and colleges, while barely 2,000 Americans study in Japan at the tertiary level, our judgment is that the current level is insufficient. Thus, urgent action is required.

4. **Much progress has been made in improving the supply of attractive opportunities for young people, both from the United States and other nations, to gain exposure to Japan**. Ten years ago there were few opportunities. But much has been done over the past several years to make study and internships in Japan more accessible.

a) At the high school level, there are many more "international" high schools in Japan that can receive American youth, and homestay programs have proliferated. Also, there is more financial support available.

b) At the collegiate level, the Japanese Ministry of Education and Culture has shown extraordinary vigor:

(1) It is providing many new scholarships for foreign youth seeking study-abroad opportunities in Japan (generous scholarships are available for about 2,000 incoming students annually). Also, there has been an increase in scholarships for degree-seeking students and graduate students.

(2) Study-abroad programs have been established not only in private universities, but also recently in several of Japan's leading national universities.

(3) Infrastructure obstacles such as the availability of international offices in universities, international student housing, and visa requirements are being addressed.

c) Similar improvements now make community and corporate exchanges much easier. A major new Japanese government initiative, the Fulbright Memorial Fund, will bring 5,000 U.S. K-12 teachers to Japan over the next five years.

d) While the supply of such opportunities is expanding, it is hoped that this trend will continue well into the future as, relative to other advanced nations, foreign students still represent a relatively small proportion of all students in Japanese schools and universities. For example, despite the considerable funds Japan spends to invite foreign students to Japan, their numbers and proportion are considerably smaller than in other advanced industrial societies. While foreign students make up over 5 percent of all students in most Western European universities and over 3 percent of U.S. tertiary-level students, in Japan they are only 1.5 percent. Of special concern is the insufficient number of incoming students to Japan from the United States and Western Europe.

5. **While participation in study-abroad programs is rising, the rate of increase and total numbers involved are insufficient to meet the objective need for this competence in the public and private sector.**

a) The interest of young Americans in studying abroad or, more accurately, the number seeking such opportunities, leveled off in the early '90s, perhaps in reaction to some or all of the following:

(1) the number of young people peaked—the children of the baby boom were succeeded by a smaller age cohort;

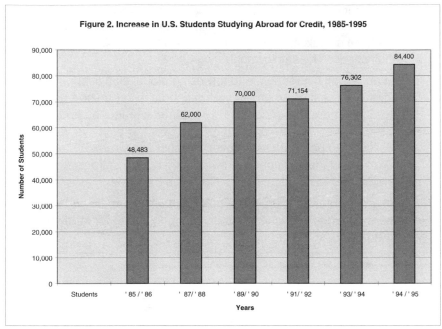

Figure 2. Increase in U.S. Students Studying Abroad for Credit, 1985-1995

Source: Open Doors 1995/1996: Report on International Educational Exchange, 1996. Todd M.Davis, ed., New York: Institute of International Education.

(2) the increasing burdens of curricular requirements, collegiate expenses, and associated part-time jobs may deter some students from study abroad;

(3) current study abroad programs may not feature the types of experiences that the pragmatic youth of the 1990s desire. As illustrated below, there is a steady increase in the proportion of study-abroad students who seek opportunities in technical fields

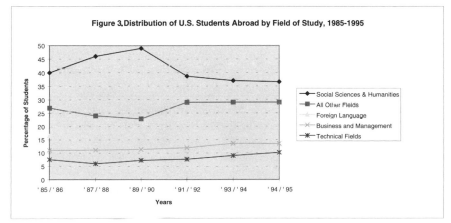

Figure 3. Distribution of U.S. Students Abroad by Field of Study, 1985-1995

Source: Open Doors 1994/1995: Report on International Educational Exchange, 1995. Todd M. Davis, ed., New York: Institute of International Education.

and business and management—but there is a scarcity of programs offering such opportunities. And the pragmatic youth don't get signals that time spent in overseas study will improve their chances for employment.

b) But apparently in response to the rising global significance of Japan, the interest of American young people in Japan seems to be growing—more Americans study Japanese language and culture in high school (80 percent growth over the past five years) and college (30 percent growth over the past five years). Familiarity with Japan and things Japanese seems up: ramen sells better, sushi is in, and the Dodgers have Nomo as their ace.

c) While U.S. interest is up, there has been little increase in the number of young Americans actually going to Japan for study and direct experience in recent years.[3]

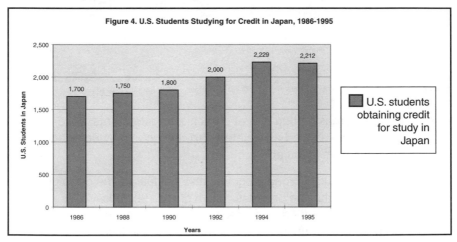

Figure 4. U.S. Students Studying for Credit in Japan, 1986-1995

Source: Open Doors 1995/1996: Report on International Educational Exchange. 1996 Todd M. Davis ed., New York: Institute of International Education

d) The U.S.-based structures for sending young people overseas may be slow in responding to the 'new' demand for transnational learning experiences:

[3] There are three sources of information on U.S. student numbers in Japan: the Laurasian Institute reports a decline based on the reports by institutions in Japan of U.S. enrollees; the Ministry of Education, which only counts students enrolled in Japanese degree programs, reports little change; IIE, which receives reports from American universities and colleges that send students to Japan, reports a modest increase. While the three approaches significantly overlap, the IIE numbers best reflect the initiatives under the direct control of U.S.-based international educators, and so they are featured here. The IIE figures are slightly larger than the others, since they capture data on students not necessarily formally enrolled in schools in Japan.

(1) At the collegiate level, the numbers who study Japanese as a ratio to those who go to Japan has over the past 10 years increased from 12/1 to 33/1.

(2) Of those who study abroad, more seek programs in business and technology and, while such programs have been expanding, there is still a grossly insufficient supply of these more pragmatic programs.

(3) In the absence of a sufficient supply of pragmatically oriented study-abroad programs, many American youth find other roads to Japan, such as through teaching jobs or as corporate interns.[4]

6. **The Japanese educational system provides Japanese young people with many of the minimum essential skills for seeking admission to U.S. schools and universities, but the Japanese system neither prepares nor sends many Japanese youth to Asia.** Few Japanese schools or universities offer courses in Asian studies and languages; it also should be emphasized that U.S. education, especially at the elementary and secondary school levels, is grossly deficient in its coverage of Asia.

7. **Both the Japanese and U.S. governments place substantial obstacles in the way of young people who seek to study in each other's country, including a time-consuming visa process and stringent limitations on the freedom of young people to work in order to support their study.** Moreover, information sources are limited and shrinking. Facilities such as the American Cultural Centers, once available in Japan to help many young Japanese as well as mature scholars to become familiar with the United States and American higher education, are facing imminent shutdowns. These facilities are highly appreciated by the Japanese public and stand as useful complements to similar facilities supported by other foreign governments that are receiving increasing numbers of Japanese students and scholars.

8. **Distinct from a focus on supply and demand, this project has engaged in a systemic analysis of international education.** This analysis has identified eight systemic principles for stimulating improvements in international education, which are described in more detail in Chapter Three.

a) Images should reflect realities

b) Information can become more accessible

---

[4] Over 2000 U.S. college graduates are in Japan each year under the JET program, where they assist Japanese public high schools in their English language education, and many more are employed by private schools. A recent study reported in the *Chronicle of Higher Education* indicates that the U.S. collegiate interest in overseas internships is considerably up.

c) Infrastructure should be built-up and unnecessary barriers lowered

d) Vertical articulation should be improved

e) Integration of key actors leads to greater impact

f) Improvements are urged in program quality

g) Internationalization can be fostered through transnational innovations

h) Beneficiaries need to be involved

9. **Application of this systemic framework points to several challenges for U.S.-Japan International Education.** For instance, there is

a) A need for a new focus on the rationale of "Transnational Competence." A new rationale is needed that fits the contemporary post-coldwar conditions of global competition and neo-localism.

Local and regional communities are exhibiting new leadership in building partnerships that steer economic, social and cultural transactions. Corporations now seek opportunities for production and sales, irrespective of national boundaries. Future citizens of the world need preparation for this emerging reality. They need a combination of technical and cultural skills suited to the particular constellations of transnational partnerships that will permeate their daily activities, both at home and at work. In short, **citizens of the 21st century need Transnational Competence**.

b) Six priority initiatives are proposed to promote this rationale:

(1) The corporate sector, as a major beneficiary (especially the information, communications, transportation, and finance sectors), should be asked both to stress the value of transnational learning experiences for employment and to provide financial support for these experiences.

(2) Every high school and college youth should have the opportunity to engage in an intensive transnational learning experience for an extended period.

(3) Transnational learning experiences should emerge from the **commitment of local communities and institutions.**

(4) Major efforts need to be devoted to **improving the quality and diversity of transnational learning experiences at all levels** (high school, college, professional/corporate, community) and to strengthening the related infrastructure.

(5) It is essential to reinforce connections between educational programs at different levels through sharing of personnel and other resources.

(6) Sustained attention should be focused on **improving the conditions for in-depth academic and scientific/technical cooperation** between Japan and the United States, with special attention to expanding the flow of information and improving the accuracy of images.

c) There is a great need for better marketing of available opportunities, possibly reinforced with new vehicles to publicize and distribute information

d) Chapters Three to Five of this report focus on these proposed initiatives and outline a number of specific actions that can be undertaken by the various participants in international education. Chapter Six offers an action agenda, drawing together the various recommendations of the report. Most of the recommendations are directed to actors in the respective nations, but several require transnational cooperation. Indeed, there are exciting opportunities for the United States and Japan to work together to create a new educational future that will benefit American and Japanese youth, while at the same time serving young people throughout the world.

Broader Implications. Japan represents only one of many environments where America and Americans will seek to expand and diversify relations. We focus on Japan because it is especially important to the United States at this historical juncture. Japan is one of America's largest trading partners and is second only to the United Kingdom in its level of investment in the United States. While the focus here is on Japan, the overall thrust of this report has, we believe, much wider applicability. The United States needs to reexamine its preparedness for participation in the emerging global society. And just as the United States takes steps to strengthen its facility in coping with Japan, so must it take steps to cope with other critical environments, especially those in East and Southeast Asia and Eastern Europe, where the opportunities are numerous but regionally-competent Americans are scarce.

Chapter One

The Need for Transnational Competence

The second half of the 20th century witnessed the transformation of the role of nation-states. Educational systems were predicated on the preservation of national boundaries, and the language of international educational exchange, in stressing the themes of national security and mutual understanding, assumed that nations were the principal actors in world affairs. Similarly, it was assumed that educational exchanges deserved the support of national governments.

Now, at the close of the century, a new era is emerging where transnational corporations, local governments, and grassroots organizations are crafting innovative networks that transcend national boundaries. These networks are becoming ever more central in everyday life, and the activities they generate surpass those organized by nation-states both in terms of volume and sustainability. As the policies and borders of nations become less distinct and the alliances between transnational corporations, nongovernmental organizations (NGOs), and sister states and cities strengthen, our prevailing assumptions about so many features of everyday life, including those guiding the field of international education, need to be reexamined.

What orientations should shape the future strategies of corporate, local, and grassroots leaders? Responding to a recent query from the RAND corporation (Bikson and Law, 1994, pp. 12-13), the chief executive officers (CEOs) of three leading U.S.-based corporations observed as follows:

> We used to be an American company operating overseas. Now we're trying to become a global company, and there's a big difference in how you think about business.

This is a different way of thinking. Everyone—in the United States and elsewhere—tends to think of his or her place as the geocenter. But national boundaries are disappearing in favor of decisions based on convenience of air connections, good telecommunications access, and the like.

It takes a cultural change. Everyone needs to have a more global economic understanding, and especially of their own individual role in the business, because everything is very competitive. We want a shared vision, down to the technician level.

And what then are the skills and aptitudes that organizations and individuals will require for their everyday life? This report argues that Transnational Competence (TNC), the thoughtful integration of technical and cultural skills, will be of increasing value in meeting the new challenges.

What is Transnational Competence?

1. Ability to imagine, analyze, and creatively address the potential of local economies/cultures

2. Knowledge of commercial/technical/cultural developments in a variety of locales

3. Awareness of key leaders (and ability to engage such leaders in useful dialogue)

4. Understanding of local customs and negotiating strategies

5. Facility in English and at least one other major language, and facility with computers

6. Technical skills in business, law, public affairs, and/or technology and awareness of their different nature in different cultural contexts

Perhaps most fundamental in transnational relations is the ability to grasp and deal with new settings. Successful players benefit from knowing who the key people are in new settings, knowing the local rules that apply to their activities, and having an understanding of local negotiating practices. Technical skills in an applied field such as engineering or law are an important component of TNC, but these need to be balanced by cultural skills to ensure effective applications. The English language is emerging as the lingua franca of many transnational relations; thus, English is an important additional component. But in many contexts English is not sufficient to ensure adequate communication, rather, other languages may be essential. Finally, often as critical as facility in a spoken language for communicating quickly and effectively is computerese.

Achieving advanced levels of TNC requires a combination of real-life experience and classroom learning. Individuals who seek TNC had best begin in high school with a serious program of language and cultural learning to complement their other studies. The high school experience should be followed by further training in college, complemented by stints of study abroad and overseas internships or other real-life international experiences. Similarly, corporations and local governments that seek to develop TNC in their workforce need to develop multi-year plans that include both (a) extended attention to the development of TNC skills and attitudes in the standing labor force, and (b) greater attention to TNC in recruitment and promotions. In sum, the acquisition of TNC is a considerable challenge and requires extended time and commitment.

This chapter stresses the need for transnational competence, both as an attribute of organizations and of the individuals who work in them. The first section reviews the trends that have given rise to the need for TNC, and the subsequent sections provide illustrations of the value of this competence for corporations, local communities, and grassroots organizations. Later chapters will review what is required to develop TNC.

The Rise of Transnationalism

Prophets of this new era point to several important trends:

Cold War and its Demise. The threat of international aggression led to a gradual expansion of the expenditures by the governments of the major industrial nations over the 1950s and 1960s, accompanied by increasing national indebtedness. By the 1970s many nations were experiencing considerable strain, leading in the early 1980s to significant reforms to reduce the size of government. Especially with the collapse of the Soviet Union, these reforms have extended to the shrinking of budgets for national defense. More generally, the politics of the leading industrial nations have come to place less reliance on national solutions, and more on local and nongovernmental approaches. National governments no longer have the funds to support major new initiatives in education and other spheres. The leadership or at least the funding will have to come from other sources, such as ambitious and/or affluent local communities, the corporate sector, and individuals.

Deregulation. From the early postwar years, the economic leaders of the free-world economies have considered various approaches to reduce trade and investment barriers through various bilateral and multilateral agreements. Perhaps the most important measure was the General Agreement of Trade and Tariffs (GATT) first proposed in 1947 and periodically reviewed since then. Economists have long preached the doctrine of comparative advantage, and these agreements represent progress in that direction not only concerning trade and overseas investment, but also currency exchange, labor migration, and other resources. In recent years, deregulation has extended to the field of education. Figures 1.1a and 1.1b, which compare recent trends in the volume of trade and investment with the size of the world economy, suggest these reforms have led to an increasing share of economic transactions that transcend national boundaries; industrial and developing countries are equally experiencing this transformation.

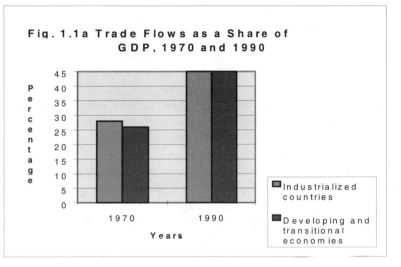

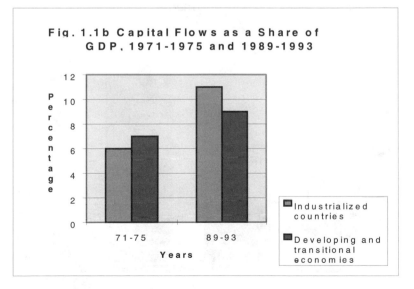

Source: World Bank, "Workers in an Integrating World," World Development Report 1995. Oxford University Press.

Knowledge Explosion. Especially since World War II, there has been an acceleration in the resources devoted to research and development in various scientific fields. This support has been rewarded by a true explosion of knowledge. The United States established its dominance in scientific productivity in the early postwar years to see its edge decline slightly from the late '70s. Regardless of the source of basic discoveries, much of this knowledge has become part of the public domain, enabling entrepreneurs around the world to convert these basic insights into marketable products. Indeed, the distribution of patents has been far more democratic than that of basic discoveries.

The expansion of research and development (R&D) has led to an institutionalization of innovation, and the rapid diffusion of technical ideas across national boundaries. Much of this diffusion occurs within the framework of transnational corporations that move their high-tech production from locale to locale to take advantage of marketing and other opportunities. While the application of technology diffuses, its generation and maintenance still tend to be concentrated in the more advanced economies where there is an adequate supply of knowledge workers. As indicated in Figure 1.2, these knowledge workers are an expanding proportion of the labor force in the United States, and they receive superior wages to workers in other sectors. The same can be said for Japan, Germany, France and other economies that have cultivated a knowledge-intensive economy.

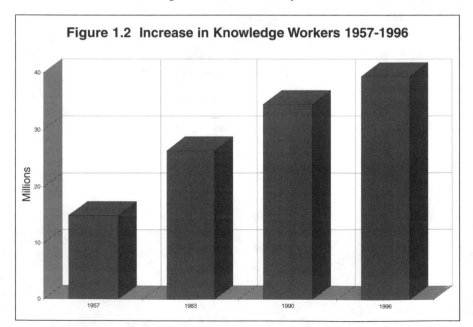

Figure 1.2 Increase in Knowledge Workers 1957-1996

Source: Cohen, W. (1996, March) Why the Chip is still the economy's champ. U.S. News and World Report *120.*

Information Explosion. Facilitating the democratization of economic opportunities has been the rapid improvement in global communication and information technology. A major contribution in recent decades has been the spread of the facsimile and the Internet, which enable virtually instant communication of new knowledge and concepts. These technologies show little respect for national boundaries. For example, the ORACLE system operates on a 24-hour basis as follows: Receiving stations are located in the United States, Britain, and Australia, and in each location most of the attendants work normal hours. Callers from around the world are routed to whatever location has an available attendant; this routing is completely transparent to the caller.

One illustration of the rapidity of the information explosion is the steady increase in the prevalence and power of computers, as illustrated in Figure 1.3. These increases are likely to continue for several decades.

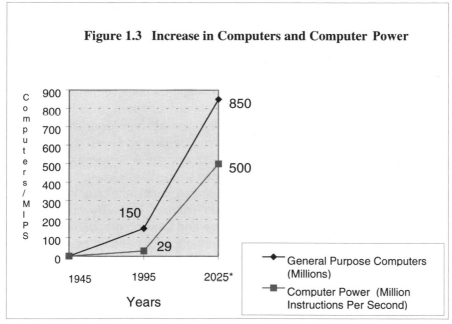

Figure 1.3 Increase in Computers and Computer Power

Source: David B. Barret, "Encyclopedia of the Future", G.T. Kurian and G.Molitor, eds., 1996, vol. 1, p. 402.

*Projections for 1995-2025 based on growth rates from 1945-1995

The Emergence of Transnational Corporations. The United States has been the pioneer in global marketing and investment. Pan American Airlines was perhaps the first major corporation to have the vision of spanning the world. Coca Cola, IBM, AMEX, and McDonalds are also known for their pioneering role in global marketing. From the 1960s, a new pattern of overseas mergers and acquisitions began to unfold with U.S., British, and even Australian firms taking the lead. The outcome has been numerous hybrid firms that combine pieces in many localities. A large transnational corporation such as AT&T claims to have operations in 181 countries. Distinct from the many instances of private-sector mergers are those such as Airbus and the Chunnel, which involve government participation. The emerging cohort of corporations is multinational, not only in capital and marketing, but also in chief officers and personnel. While transnational, most have their roots in a particular area of the world. Those anchored in the West have tended to direct most of their activities toward western markets, and those anchored in Asia often have an Asia focus. Over time, even these distinctions may disappear.

Local Responses. The geographic span of transnational organizations is extensive, and their everyday operations lead to interaction with diverse peoples and settings. Local and regional communities understand that many advantages accrue from welcoming these organizations. For example, in Buffalo, a medium-sized U.S. city, there is extensive Canadian investment, Japanese interests own a factory that produces tires and innumerable auto dealerships, a Hong Kong company owns a major bank, a Korean company owns a printing establishment, a Swedish company has a minority partnership in a machine tools plant, and so on. Many of these companies decided to locate in Buffalo because Buffalo courted them. The mayor's office and the local chamber of commerce developed a public relations program to sell the Buffalo advantage: Buffalo offers a convenient location not only for approaching the American Midwest, but also for approaching Canada and even Mexico (which is joined with the United States in NAFTA). And the American companies in Buffalo carry out business in all the places where these foreign investments have originated. The Buffalo story is repeated in city after city in the United States that seeks to become "world class" (Kanter, 1995). By virtue of these many acts of civic self-promotion, a large and growing proportion of today's transactions are carried out with little concern for national borders. While cities usually court transnational opportunities with targeted trade missions, it is increasingly common for state and regional governments to have more permanent agencies to nurture these opportunities; for example, about one-third of the U.S. states now have international trade offices which deploy trade representatives in leading cities around the world. Those locales that seek relations seem to get them. One commentator has proposed the term "glocalization" to describe this wedding of local initiative and global processes.

The Long Arm of Nongovernmental Organizations. Just as corporations have come to operate on a global scale, so have many of the new organizations concerned with pressing social issues such as environmental preservation, drug prevention, child survival, and human rights.

These organizations, sometimes referred to as nongovernmental organizations (NGOs), find they need to operate globally as the issues they address do not respect national boundaries. UNICEF is one key transnational organization to attempt this shift; UNICEF's primary mission is child survival, which it addresses through strategies of locally-based efforts related to community health, nutrition packages, inoculation, and basic education. But in recent years, UNICEF has discovered that the welfare of many children is endangered by international epidemics or international rings of adoption and child prostitution, so increasing proportions of the organization's funds have come to be devoted to transnational units that investigate and address these processes. Amnesty International, Greenpeace, and CARE are other examples of NGOs that deploy on a global scale to address issues that transcend national boundaries. While UNICEF was created as an international agency by its parent organization (the United Nations), Amnesty International began as a U.S. organization and Greenpeace began as a local one; yet all now are transnational in strategy and operation. These NGOs contribute to a new global safety net, complementing the work of intergovernmental organizations such as the World Trade Organization and the International Court.

What is Required to Nurture a Transnational Presence: The Corporate Example

The expanding network of transnational connections prompts new behavior and opens up new options for all involved players. In that the corporate sector has tended to take the lead in transnationalism, we must first consider how this trend has influenced corporate strategic thinking.

Corporations that seek to increase their presence in foreign markets have a number of options. In foreign markets that do not have similar products, the focus may be on market research to identify unique aspects of local taste. Following that, the corporation may simply export products or take the more adventurous step of entering into a joint venture or even setting up a local subsidiary.

However, in many foreign markets the challenges are more substantial as local producers already have competitive products on the market. Where there is local competition, entering corporations may devote considerable effort to obtain an understanding of the latest production techniques or marketing approaches used by local firms. Depending on corporate strategy, one or more of the responsible divisions within the corporation will take the lead in exploring the overseas settings. Any of several practices may be considered:

1. The simplest practice is to **obtain information** about the practices of foreign competitors through studying annual reports, trade journals, technical

literature, and other sources. This practice requires analytical ability, the foundation component of TNC, as well as technical expertise, the sixth component.

2. **Visits to foreign settings** to review new technical information and to discuss product ideas is a somewhat more complicated initiative, as it requires the development of contacts and scheduling. This practice requires an ability to analyze the potential of diverse economies and locales as well as knowledge of particular commercial and technical developments, the second component of TNC.

3. **Recruiting international staff** tends to enhance a firm's ability to understand and operate in a foreign setting; the international staff is likely to have both firsthand familiarity with foreign practices and a network of local contacts on which to draw in carrying out business in the foreign setting. This practice is enhanced by an understanding of who counts in the target setting, the third component of TNC.

4. **Investing in foreign technologies or firms** is another way to gain insight as the investment is frequently associated with the transfer of technology and staff. An understanding of local negotiating strategies, the fourth component of TNC, should facilitate success in these endeavors.

5. **Establishing foreign subsidiaries** is a relatively expensive measure as it requires a mastery of foreign land and tax laws and the recruitment and posting of appropriate staff in the foreign setting; however, such a measure is usually required if a corporation is to gain a major foothold in the foreign setting. The ability to use the local language, the fifth component of TNC, is essential for carrying out business in the local setting, as are technical skills and awareness of their nature in different cultural contexts.

Table 1.1 Nurturing a Transnational Presence:
A Comparison of Strategies

Strategies	Requires Foreign Help	Requires Funds	U.S. is Active	Japan is Active
Obtain Information	Low	Low	Low	High
Foreign Visits	Moderate	Moderate	Low	High
Recruit International Staff	Low	Moderate	High	Moderate
Invest in Foreign Companies/ Technology	High	High	Low	High
Establish Foreign Subsidiaries	Moderate	High+	Moderate	High

Reviewing these options, it becomes obvious that the out-of-country presence of a corporation is only a fraction of the total impact of transnational linkages. Each of these practices requires the skills and insights of the individual employees of the interested firm, though in different ways. The first requires headquarters employees to learn more while staying put in their home office. The second requires headquarters employees to travel. The third, fourth and fifth require some headquarters employees to relocate to foreign settings, where they will be expected to interact according to foreign customs. All of these practices may also lead to the recruitment of new staff who have special coping skills in foreign settings; an option here is to favor nationals from the country that hosts the main headquarters for the company's operations (a tendency of Japanese firms and some U.S. firms, such as Motorola), or natives of the sites where the subsidiaries are located.

Regardless of the choice, the employees involved in these activities require Transnational Competence.

Transnationalism in Japan and Asia

While U.S. multinationals were setting the pace in the 1950s and 1960s, the economies of Asia were pulling themselves out of a deep economic hole created by the Second World War and its aftershocks in the Chinese communist revolution, the war on the Korean peninsula, and the war in Vietnam. Japan began its race to economic fame in the 1960s with its "Doubling Income Plan," which saw Japanese industry rapidly expand its production and exports in steel, shipbuilding, machine goods, and electrical and electronic products. The initial stages of Japan's economic rise were built on a combination of nationally directed trade and industrial policy.

A special characteristic of Japanese economic organization is groups of allied firms (known as *keiretsu*), each built around a major bank such as Fuji, Mitsubishi, Mitsui, and so on. An important component of most of these groups is their trading house, a firm with offices around the world to facilitate international transactions for the group. Through the prowess of the trading houses, Japanese exports rapidly expanded during the '60s, enabling Japan to capture important shares of world trade in textiles, steel, and shipbuilding. By the late 1960s Japan was making major gains in electrical and electronic products, as well as automobiles.

While government initially provided the lead for Japan Inc., in more recent years the corporations have shown greater independence. Many of the corporations have achieved mammoth status. Of the ten largest banks in the world, seven are Japanese (Besher, 1991, p. 221). According to *Fortune*, five of the top 25 on the list of the world's largest manufacturing corporations have a Japanese pedigree (Besher, 1991, p. 84). While the marketing scope of these corporations is global, their control is firmly in Japan. In most instances, all of the members of the boards of directors are Japanese nationals. While most list their stocks on public stock exchanges, including the New York Stock Exchange, they have shown a remarkable ability to resist foreign take-over bids.

Japan's global corporations have had a reputation for keeping their core technologies in Japan and limiting their offshore operations to assembly plants and sales. With the core technologies protected on Japan's shores, the firms devolved little authority to their offshore operations. Nevertheless, the top people in these offshore operations were usually Japanese nationals, to ensure close communication with the central office. Relative to European and American multinationals, Japanese multinationals have tended to have a larger number of representatives from the home company in their overseas operations.[5] But through the mid-1980s, a young Japanese executive was reluctant to go overseas, as it implied exile from the heart of corporate life (M. White, 1988).

SONY's Transnational Orientation Aided its Growth

Key to SONY Corporation's phenomenal growth has been its early appreciation of the power of a transnational strategy. Whereas most Japanese electronics firms trace their origins to at least the 1930s, SONY was founded in the 1950s by an innovative group of engineers who decided to focus on the international market. From its earliest days, SONY sought employees who had exceptional skills, both in their technical specialties and in foreign languages. By the mid-1960s, SONY had a promising line of electronic products on the shelves of many stores in the U.S. and Western Europe, and more than 60 percent of its sales were outside of Japan. In contrast to SONY were such traditional Japanese electrical and electronics firms as TOSHIBA and Mitsubushi Denki, which targeted local markets. By the early 1980s, SONY with its transnational strategy had surpassed TOSHIBA in sales, and by the mid-1990s was approaching gigantic Mitsubushi Denki. In 1996, Mitsubushi Denki announced its new VISION 21, declaring that it now intended to become a "Transnational Firm" and that all future international communication would be in English. But alas, the announcement was released to the press in Japanese only.

---

[5] A recent survey of the Japan Overseas Enterprises Association (JOEA), a grouping of more than 500 Japanese corporations with overseas manufacturing plants, reports that the percentage of expatriates in Japanese overseas branches was nearly 20 times higher than for European and American firms. Only 20 percent of Japanese overseas subsidiaries were run by locals (Kawakami, 1996, p. 44).

28

The overseas strategy of Japanese corporations, involving a heavy dependence on overseas Japanese and strict limits on the sharing of technology, set limits on the scope of Japanese overseas expansion. So in recent years, Japan's global corporations have introduced significant shifts in their overseas strategy. These include a greater reliance on foreign nationals, extending greater autonomy to the managers of overseas operations, and allowing more advanced technology to be used in offshore production. Moreover, during the 1980s, Japanese firms began to establish many overseas research and development institutes.

Of special interest has been the effort to increase the prestige attached to overseas assignments for Japanese nationals. Many such assignments are now described as promotions by personnel officers. Official publications of various industrial associations spotlight the activities of key overseas managers. Similarly, economic newspapers note that many of the individuals now being selected as CEOs have spent significant proportions of their careers overseas. Perhaps of greatest importance is the recent policy statement by NIKKEIREN, the All Japan Employers Association, that foreign language skills and multicultural sensitivity should be important criteria in the selection of recruits for member corporations. All in all, Japanese corporations have developed a more consistent policy than have U.S. corporations for encouraging transnational competence.

The corporations of other Asian nations are less heralded than those of Japan, partly because they are usually smaller in scale. The partial exception is Korea, where there are several mammoth multinationals that occupy a major role in world steel production, shipbuilding, construction, and semiconductors. Also, several Korean firms are achieving some success in exporting automobiles. The primary direction of trade for many of the Asian countries has been with other Asian countries. But particularly in the past decade, as Japan has moved more of its production offshore, the direction of trade has shifted to the United States and Europe. Relative to Japan, far larger proportions of Korean, Taiwanese, and Hong Kong youth have pursued advanced education in the West (primarily in the United States). The major theme in recent educational reform in Korea and Taiwan has been to prepare the respective labor forces for the emerging global economy. Reforms include a renewed stress on both technical skills and the English language (in future, to be initiated from grade three of the primary school). It may be that these nations have a deeper understanding of the United States than does Japan.

U.S.-Japan Interactions in the Transnational Economy

While many U.S. corporations have been pioneers in the trend toward forging multinational modes of operating, much of their energy has focused on Western Europe and Latin America. They have tended, until recently, to downplay the potential of Asia both as a market and as a locus of creativity and product development.[6] In contrast, Japanese corporations, while attentive to Asian opportunities, have placed considerable emphasis on the U.S. setting. The relative competitiveness of U.S. and Japanese firms vis-a-vis each other can be illustrated by their respective success in comprehending each other's research and development strategies.

For a variety of reasons, Japanese corporations are likely to be more familiar with technical and commercial opportunities in the United States than vice versa. Japan until the past decade has viewed itself as behind the United States in technical capability, and thus has devoted extensive resources to information-gathering and educational/technical exchanges in an effort to catch up. Even as Japan has caught up, it has continued to devote resources to human and information exchange. In contrast, the United States has believed it has little to learn from Japan; thus, the two nations' approaches are asymmetric. The differences can be compared in terms of the practices discussed above for "nurturing a transnational presence":

1. *Obtain Information.* In order to catch up, the Japanese government has placed high priority on finding out what is going on in other nations. From the mid-1950s a special government agency, the Japan Information Center for Science and Technology (JICST), was established to translate key international material. Currently it receives and translates abstracts of more than 5,000 titles of foreign research each month, offering interested researchers access to this material (Bloom, 1990, pp.22ff). From the mid-1980s the abstracts were placed on computer tapes and made accessible to researchers throughout Japan from a number of regional access stations. In recent years, access has been expanded through reliance on the Internet system, so virtually any university laboratory can review current research. The system now also includes the abstracts of most current Japanese research.

No comparable system exists in the United States for tracking Japanese research (or for that matter, research of any other foreign system). A small proportion of Japanese articles (those published with English-language ab-

---

[6] A number of large U.S. corporations actually closed down their Asia operations during or after World War II, concluding that Asia would be too impoverished to constitute a significant market. Even today, many U.S. corporate leaders believe that America has a monopoly on creativity, and that Asian engineers are unlikely to come up with significant technical innovations.

stracts) are included in major systems such as the Chemical Abstracts, but most fields do not include Japanese material. From the late 1980s, agencies such as University Microfilms and the National Technical Information Service began to collect abstracts of selected Japanese articles, and more recently several JICST terminals have been set up in the United States. But the scale of these activities is still somewhat limited.

2. *Foreign Visits.* Japan sends more corporate "researchers" overseas than it receives; in 1991, the respective numbers were 146,000 sent to 84,000 received. Japan sent 47.5 percent of its researchers going overseas to the United States, while American researchers made up only 6.2 percent of those received by Japan (STA, 1992, p.10). In other words, approximately 72,000 Japanese researchers visited the United States, compared to 5,200 U.S. researchers who visited Japan.

3. *Recruit International Staff.* A recent concern of Japanese corporations has been to internationalize their workforce through hiring more foreign employees, particularly for R&D roles (Nakayama, 1994). Japanese corporate leaders see this as one way of responding to the United States demand for greater access to Japanese corporate laboratories. In contrast, for many decades United States corporations have hired foreign-born researchers, drawing primarily on the large pool who received advanced training in American universities (National Science Board, 1993, pp.82-83; Finn, 1996, p.108). While this strategy has worked well in the past, in view of improvements in working conditions outside the United States and more stringent U.S. regulations on technical training and immigration, it may become increasingly difficult to induce the best and brightest foreigners to accept U.S. jobs; a reverse "brain drain" has been reported for Asian scholars (Choi, 1995).

4. *Invest in Foreign Companies and Technologies.* Japan also buys more technology than it sells, while the reverse is true of the United States. Technology trade is typically measured in terms of the amount of licensing payments for the year (both for old and new contracts). In the Japanese case, there are two different accountings of these amounts; the more generous accounting suggests that Japan's sales, which once were quite modest, now nearly equal its purchases. Over the last 20 years Japan's sales have increased 1,800 percent suggesting a rapid surge in the quality of Japanese technology. In the U.S. case, sales have always been high and in 1991 were four times as large as U.S. purchases; moreover, U.S. sales were several times that of Japanese sales.

5. *Establish Foreign Subsidiaries.* Japanese corporations over the 1980s set up numerous affiliations with the research units of U.S. firms. Also, Japanese corporations established many independent research laboratories in the United States to take advantage of U.S.- trained research talent, as well as to build linkages with U.S. university-based researchers. A 1992 study by the U.S.

31

Department of Commerce indicates there were 476 Japanese corporations with U.S.-based R&D subsidiaries (Commerce, 1992). While the rapid growth of the Japanese presence has surprised U.S. observers, it should be pointed out that a number of U.S. corporations have had bases in Japan for several decades; a 1991 NSF survey indicates 75 U.S. companies have an R&D presence in Japan, and others have plans to establish a presence.

This review of the evidence suggests that the Japanese corporate world is taking advantage of far more opportunities to become familiar with U.S. technical developments than is the United States vis-a-vis Japan. Key in the Japanese strategy is the mobilization of employees who have a high level of transnational competence, especially in relation to the U.S. market.

The Impact of Transnational Competence

These differences in technical strategy underlie the relative success of U.S. and Japan-based corporations in penetrating each other's markets. Numerous Japanese corporations have taken the trouble to develop a U.S.-oriented strategy, including the deployment of appropriately prepared personnel, while relatively few U.S. corporations have reciprocated. But as we turn to other parts of the world, the picture becomes more complicated.

For example, while Japan's approach to transnational competence has prepared it well for U.S. relations, it is not notably well-prepared for Asian interactions. Japanese schools and universities give virtually no attention to Asian languages and far less attention to Asian culture and history than they devote to the West. Similarly, the major thrust in U.S. preparation, whether in the school system or corporations, is toward Western Europe. Thus, both Japan and the U.S. share the common weakness of poor preparation for Asia-oriented transactions.

This common weakness is surprising when one considers the shifting pattern of global trade as illustrated in Figure 1.4. In the mid-1980s, Western Europe was the U.S.'s largest trading partner, and Japan had the U.S. as its foremost trading partner. But by the mid-1990s, the direction of trade for both nations had significantly shifted to East Asia. East Asia was No. 1 for both the United States and Japan.

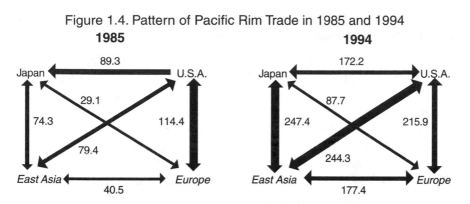

Figure 1.4. Pattern of Pacific Rim Trade in 1985 and 1994

Note: East Asia includes Korea, Taiwan, Hong Kong, China, and the ASEAN nations; the figures are the sum of imports and exports in units of U.S. billion dollars.

Source: IMF, *Direction of Trade Statistics Yearbook,* various issues.

Figure 1.4 focuses on aggregate trade, but as one looks into the direction of trade it turns out that **both** Japan and the United States currently run trade deficits with East Asia. In the United States there was much lamenting of the large trade deficit with Japan, but as the Japanese trade deficit stabilized, the imbalances with Taiwan, and especially China, steadily increased. Some say this is because Japan shifted its business to these areas, but that is at best half the story. U.S.-based transnationals have also shifted much of their production to China and other Asian sites (Holloway, 1996). And at the same time, many new Asian firms have emerged to focus on overseas export opportunities. In other words, the East Asian nations may have a better insight into the markets of Japan and the United States than vice versa.

While Figure 1.4 treats nations as units, in terms of contemporary trade relations it is often more appropriate to think in terms of local, rather than national, strengths. The eastern seaboard of the United States, where the nation was born, has long historical ties with Western Europe; many of its residents trace their origins to the United Kingdom, France, Germany, and Italy. Their children often study these languages in school. Their communities do well in trade with mostly European markets, as indicated by the essentially even terms of trade with that region. But the eastern seaboard has much weaker links with Asia, and its exports to Asia are modest relative to Asian imports. America's western states, by way of contrast, carry on vigorous and more or less balanced trade with Asia. And America's Southwest, where many Americans trace their ancestry to Latin America, does well in trade with the Spanish-speaking nations to the south.

The American Problem: The Gap Between What Should be Done and What is Being Done to Promote TNC

American-based corporations, being the leaders in transnational expansion, have weighed these options for several decades. As time has passed, increasing proportions of those individuals chosen for top positions in the most successful American-based firms have themselves had an extensive track record in international business. It is common for these top business leaders to stress the importance of language and cultural skills as an essential component in the preparation for business careers; consider these opinions of top executives reported in a recent RAND study (Bikson and Law, 1994, p. 25):

> Companies will do much better if they insist that their employees learn the local language and customs. This definitely translates into a competitive advantage.

> Americans need to know more about the rest of the world if they want to do business in it.

> The inability to perform cross-culturally will soon become a failure criterion.

These sentiments have been echoed in numerous reports and studies. As early as 1979 the Presidential Commission on Foreign Language and International Studies found that "one of the leading reasons behind a declining U.S. international competitive edge was American business' lack of foreign language and area expertise" (Beamish and Calof, 1989, p. 554). Fifield et al. (1990), in a National Occupational Education Survey, report that many businesses list international curricula as a high priority. Similarly, Gersterner (June 5, 1994) reports that major sectors of the business community are demanding the internationalization of the labor force.

While many books and reports have been written echoing these messages, it remains that few U.S. corporations have a consistent policy for their international operations. A gap is apparent between the perspectives of top executives in U.S. firms and the practices of the human resource management specialists. Lawler, Cohen and Chang (1993) note that these specialists do not incorporate "global competition and the state of the economy into their evaluative process." They often are isolated from the core business priorities of their corporations.

Thus, while top executives might prefer a more internationally minded workforce, the personnel officers typically are oblivious to this interest. In recruitment and promotions, they focus on technical skills and the teamwork displayed at the home work site. For example, a recent Conference Board Report (1996), observing that repatriation practice is an indicator of sound international personnel policy, concludes that European firms are outstanding in this regard. In contrast, the majority of U.S. companies surveyed had not informed their overseas expatriates of their next assignment within four months of their return, and fully 87 percent reported that the majority of returning expatriates did not receive a promotion upon return. The international dimension is ignored.

One possible explanation for the parochial practices of the human resource officers has been the increasing tendency for American multinationals to rely primarily on foreign nationals for overseas work. The multinationals find that it is extremely expensive to place an American in an overseas post, ranging from two to four times the cost of keeping the American at home. Under that circumstance, the U.S.-based multinationals favor hiring locally for their overseas operations. For example, there are only a handful of Americans among the 3,000 employees of IBM Japan.

U.S. Firms Often Chose Foreign Born Employees For Key Transnational Positions

Discussing the recent U.S. upsurge in Asian investment, the Far Eastern Economic Review recently focused on David Wang, national executive for GE International's operations in Malaysia, Singapore, and Brunei.

Wang was born 52 years ago in China and attended kindergarten in Shanghai, high school in Jakarta, and obtained an engineering degree at a university in St. Louis, Missouri. After running the family business in Indonesia for three years, he returned to the United States and in 1980 joined General Electric as a product engineer. A decade later, the firm tapped his Mandarin language skills by moving him to Beijing, where he led the negotiations to establish GE Hangwei Medical Systems, GE's first equity joint venture in the Middle Kingdom. And in August 1995, Wang was re-assigned to Kuala Lumpur to lead the company's initiatives in Malaysia, Singapore, Brunei, and Vietnam, where his fluency in Malay and Cantonese will come in handy. "The most important reason why they picked me was my ability to manage manufacturing in a cross-cultural environment," says Wang. (Holloway, 1996, p. 40)

But even if a transnationally oriented company relies primarily on foreign-born employees or foreign nationals for their overseas posts, there still are many international tasks at the home site. Returning to the list of options introduced in the previous section, we see that home-based employees will be expected to obtain and analyze international information, supply foreign sites with various goods and services, and visit foreign sites periodically to review operations and evaluate new opportunities. In sum, there are many activities for the home-based workforce that require transnational competence.

One of the studies commissioned for this report projects a rapid increase in the requirement for TNC if the U.S. labor force is to remain competitive.[7] The expansion of the level of Transnational Competence of the U.S. labor force will require considerable effort on the part of schools and universities, but these institutions will not exert that effort until they receive strong positive signals from the corporate sector. Regrettably, the challenge of upgrading America's TNC is not acknowledged by the personnel officers of most U.S.-based transnational corporations. These officers hire for today's needs, not for those five years out.

Universal Competence or Transnational Competence?

Comparing recent pronouncements of political and corporate leaders in the United States and Asia, it might be said that two different views are being articulated. On the one hand is the culture-free or universalistic position, which sees the world as an undifferentiated global market where various local settings can be reached through a skillful application of technical and managerial skills; cultural and language skills are not stressed. This view, most often articulated by Americans, notes America's preeminent position in the world economy; American business practices are emulated around the world. English is the lingua franca of international commerce. Thus to succeed in international transactions, all that is required is to speak slower, listen more carefully, practice a proper level of courtesy and sensitivity. As Nike says, "Just Do It". The universalistic approach to global marketing is symbolized by Michael Jordan jumping over the Eiffel Tower and then over the Great Wall in his $200 all-sport wonder shoes.

The counterview, which might be called the culture-full or transnational position, says things must be more complicated. There is always an important

---

[7] This study attempted an analysis of the future demand for transnational competence in the U.S. labor force (Ilon and Paulino, 1996). Using conservative assumptions, this analysis suggests the demand for internationally trained employees will rise from 973,000 in 1996 to 1,649,000 in 2005, an increase of 70 percent. This represents an annual growth rate of six percent or 75,000 new internationally trained employees each year. The rate of growth in the demand for employees that excel in transnational competence far exceeds any projection for the overall expansion of the labor force.

cultural element. An early expression of this view was Senator Paul Simon's observation that, "You can buy in any language, but you can only sell in the language the consumer understands." While this second view is not prevalent in the United States, it is much more widely accepted outside the United States.

Pierre Bismuth and Henry Edmundson of Schlumberger, Limited, point out that their corporation hires internationally, and is looking for people who can "survive and flourish in the type of multi-cultural environment in which we conduct our business." In addition, for non-English speakers, this policy means acquisition of English, and for English speakers it usually means eventual acquisition of at least one other language. Schlumberger categorizes its employees in terms of their mobility: (a) mobile only within their home country; (b) can work anywhere, but remain residents of one country; (c) can move a few times with their families as part of their career development; (d) are fully mobile with their families, available for any assignment. The expectation is that most senior managers will be drawn from (d). It is clear that student exchange programs alone cannot create more of category (d), but they can and should contribute to the potential pool of such flexible professionals.

The culture-free view is premised on a solid truth that English is the lingua franca, and for many places it is sufficient. Also, American business practices are more and more accepted. For Americans, this makes things easy for most purposes. They may not need to put as much effort into acquiring Transnational Competence as their foreign counterparts in that many of the traits of this competence are American-born. For non-Americans it means they expect to profit from learning the American way—so it is not surprising that many foreigners come to America essentially to learn how to do things the American way.

But there are limits to the reach of an English-only strategy. Americans have discovered this in Japan and China, where the market has proved tough to penetrate. Laws are different, the bureaucracy is stubborn, the distribution system is cumbersome, and the negotiating customs are subtle. A majority of the successful heads of U.S. businesses in Japan and China are headed by Americans who have both technical and cultural skills. [8] Eastern Europe is also likely to prove a tough market to crack for Americans, for many of the same reasons as in East Asia. Walt Disney's difficulties in starting a French Disneyland suggest that U.S. technique may not be sufficient to succeed even in

[8] A study of expatriate managers sent to Japan reports that 90 percent were given significantly less successful ratings compared to their immediately prior assignment (Seward, 1975); another study reports that 80 percent of the expatriate managers in Japan were considered failures by their headquarters (Adams, 1969). In both these studies, those managers with Japanese language skills were more likely to be successful.

France; the Disneyland example indicates that the nature of a product, in this case a culturally loaded entertainment experience, may have as much bearing on marketing success as the characteristics of the local business settings.

Of course, American corporations are not alone in encountering difficulty in foreign settings. Japanese companies find it relatively easy going in North America, Latin America, and parts of Asia. They face a tougher business environment in Europe; the Middle East and Africa are reported to pose even greater challenges. Japanese firms even encounter significant obstacles in Korea and China, because their representatives fail to adhere to local customs in negotiations. A major constraint on Japanese business is their adoption of English as the international business language, whereas in many overseas settings other languages (French, Arabic, Spanish, Portuguese, Chinese, and the various languages of Southeast Asia, which are not stressed in Japanese education) would serve them better. So it can be concluded that the nature of the transaction has a bearing on the efficacy of the two views. Many transactions are challenging and require culture-full Transnational Competence.

A sensible compromise between these two views is to observe that the culture-free approach may work for the easy areas. On the other hand, the culture-full approach is essential for the tough areas. And for the U.S., the tough areas are Japan, China, the Middle East, and Eastern Europe. For Japan, the U.S. is easy, but other parts of the world are tough. Where the going is tough, the culture-full approach, or Transnational Competence, is the answer.

Conclusion: Who Benefits and Who Should Support TNC

At the close of the 20th century, a new global system is emerging that transcends nation-states. By virtue of a range of multilateral agreements achieved over the past several decades and improvements in communications technology, the shield of national protectionist policies is weakening, allowing the pace of global competition to accelerate.

Similarly overseas investment is expanding more rapidly than domestic investment. There is a significant increase in the flow of international workers, whether as domestic servants, construction workers, or medical personnel.

This shift in the global order offers both hope and uncertainty. Hope derives from the perception of peace and greater long-term stability, hence the possibility of a new era of development and prosperity. But uncertainty derives from the future locus of development. National influence is weakening. Local areas in Southern China, Jakarta, and Silicon Valley prosper—at least for awhile— as the goods and services they specialize in find a promising niche in the global marketplace, while other areas such as America's great midwestern Rustbelt or Japan's Shikoku decline. Will the future be at home or abroad, in this neighborhood or elsewhere? Local leadership will be critical: "Think globally and act locally" will be the password to prosperity. Those who fail to develop an informed strategy for participating in the global economy are likely to experience the harsh reality of corporate downsizing and closures, with the associated pain of reductions in public revenues and services.

An important component of successful local responses will be the development of strategic transnational economic and political linkages—Wisconsin's courting of Ajinomoto and northern Kyushu's recent success with semiconductors are two such examples. These local responses build on many elements including natural resources, transportation capabilities and other infrastructures, and a favorable business climate. Among the most critical elements, in the view of this study, is the presence of Transnational Competence, the ability to collect and analyze information about relevant opportunities wherever they be, and then to translate those opportunities into action. In the words of U.S. Secretary of Labor Robert Reich:

> We are living through a transformation that will rearrange the politics and economics of the coming century. There will be no *national* products or technologies, no national corporations, no national industries. There will no longer be national economies as we have come to understand that concept. All that will remain rooted within national borders are the people who comprise a nation. Each nation's primary assets will be its citizens' skills and insights. Each nation's primary political task will be to cope with the centrifugal forces of the global economy, which tear at the ties binding citizens together— bestowing ever greater wealth on the most skilled and insightful, while consigning the less skilled to a declining standard of living. (Reich,1991, p.3)

Drawing on the examples of the United States and Japan, two nations that have had almost diametrically opposed experiences over the past half century, this study seeks to understand the nature of Transnational Competence and what needs to be done to develop it. While the focus is on these two nations and their citizens, the goal is to increase understanding of a challenge that confronts all citizens of the emerging global village.

In this chapter we have outlined the economic forces behind transnationalism and the broad implications of this trend for the way future citizens of the world will live and work. Many observers conclude that future citizens and workers will need to acquire Transnational Competence in order to thrive in this new world. International education has an important role to play in promoting Transnational Competence. In the next chapters, we will consider how education has to be changed to address this essential need. Our focus is on the United States and Japan, but we think the lessons are broader.

Chapter Two

The Peripheral Status of International Education

Success in fostering Transnational Competence will be influenced by current educational practice, especially in the curricula for foreign languages, social studies, and area studies (which, in combination with educational exchanges, are known as international education). In this chapter, we first highlight several key similarities and differences in United States and Japanese educational practice, and then turn to the two nations' approaches to international education. We conclude, for both national contexts, that international education occupies a relatively peripheral status and, moreover, that the goals and structures of many international programs were intended for an earlier era. However, there are important signs of change, especially in Japan, which we will highlight.

The Current Practice of Education in the U.S. and Japan

Building the Nation. Given the prominence of the United States and Japan in world affairs, we sometimes forget how young these two nations are. The United States emerged as the "First New Nation" following the revolutionary war at the end of the 18th century; the Meiji Restoration establishing modern Japan occurred in 1868. As these new nations emerged, their leaders expressed concern about building a strong sense of national identity. The United States faced the challenge of Americanizing successive waves of immigrants, most of whom spoke little English. And Japan faced the challenge of homogenizing the cultural and linguistic differences that had been cultivated over several centuries by the respective feudal domains (han) that had lived in forced isolation from each other.

Thus in both settings, the educational authorities placed a somewhat exceptional stress on national language and national history. Also, in order to catch up with the powerful nations of Western Europe, considerable stress was placed on mathematics and science. At first, foreign languages were required in the United States, but gradually these requirements were relaxed and the proportion of young Americans taking a foreign language declined. Japan, conscious of the need to acquire "western science" in order to catch up with the West, has historically placed a greater emphasis on foreign languages, making English and at least one other foreign language a requirement at the secondary level; however, as in the case of the United States, this requirement has relaxed somewhat over time.

The European Precedent. At the time these two new nations were emerging, European education was already well developed. The United States, as a former colony of England, tended to draw on English precedent in developing its educational practice. Thus, as in the case of England, the principal decisions on such matters as curriculum, textbooks, and the selection of personnel and students were left to local educational authorities and even to individual schools. The American commitment to decentralization has led to significant variation between states, and even between the districts within state systems. As one example illustrates (Table 2.1), a few U.S. states place considerable stress on foreign languages at the secondary level, while the majority place little or no emphasis on this subject matter. As in other educational matters in the United States, efforts to improve the quality of international education will depend largely on state-level initiatives.

Table 2.1
Percentage of Students in High School Districts That Require Two or More Years of a Foreign Language for Graduation (by State) 1990-91

States That Lead in Foreign Language		States Where Foreign Language Is Not Emphasized	
District of Columbia	100.0%	Alaska	0.0%
New York	77.8%	Delaware	0.0%
Rhode Island	60.4%	Hawaii	0.0%
California	57.5%	North Dakota	0.0%
West Virginia	24.3%	Nevada	0.2%
Tennessee	23.7%	North Carolina	0.6%
Massachusetts	23.6%	Indiana	0.8%

Source: U.S. Department of Education, National Center for Education Statistics, Condition of Education 1994.

In the early stages of developing its modern educational system, Japan surveyed all of the educational systems of Western Europe as well as of the United States. Moreover, it invited several foreign advisers to assist in the early planning, notably David Murray of Rutgers University in New Jersey. While Japan expressed much interest in American education, it finally outlined a new system that borrowed many of its principal features from France.

Thus, the Japanese system is much more highly centralized, with most curricular decisions made in Tokyo. Guidelines for textbook selection and teacher recruitment are also drafted in Tokyo. In the years immediately after World War II, when the United States led the Allied Occupation of Japan, many Americanizing reforms were introduced to Japanese education, including a greater local role in educational decision-making. However, due to later counter-reforms, the basic pattern of centralized control was not fundamentally altered. The more centralized character of Japanese education means that change is heavily dependent on decisions by Ministry of Education bureaucrats and national politicians.

Possibly derived from these differences in educational tradition is the greater concern of U.S. education with supporting individual development, whereas Japanese education places more emphasis on a uniform outcome for all students. The individualistic character of American education is expressed through such innovations as special education and education for gifted children. Also, U.S. education offers young people many choices both in terms of school and tracks within schools, as well as in the selection of particular courses within these parameters. Japanese young people have fewer choices.

Strong Foundation or a Strong Finish. Japan's modern leaders sensed that education was to be the key to their nation's modernization, so only four years after the Meiji Restoration in 1872, they pledged their commitment to universal education. Impressive effort was devoted to developing a coherent program of basic education so that within 30 years, essentially all Japanese young people were enrolled. Only as the basic level was being completed did the leaders began to initiate major improvements at the secondary and tertiary level.

In contrast to Japan's stress on basic education, the concern in colonial America to explore more deeply the wisdom of God and to train pastors to spread the gospel led to the establishment of many small colleges and seminaries. Harvard College was founded in 1634, Yale by 1676; by the time of the revolution there were some 80 institutions of higher education, and by the middle of the 19th century more than 800. Local business leaders were often supporters of these institutions, believing that a local college added dignity to their community, and with the Morill Land-grant Act state governments also became supporters of a new type of college focusing on the agricultural and mechanical sciences. **The American enthusiasm for colleges has often seemed to exceed its enthusiasm for those educational institutions providing basic education**. Certainly as time has passed, the United States has created the largest and most diversified system of higher education in the world, and it spends a greater proportion of its GNP on these institutions than does any other contemporary society. It might be said that the major break in American education is between school education and tertiary education, whereas in many other societies, including Japan the major divide is between lower- and upper-secondary education.

School-Work Links are Weak. In both nations, governments for largely political ends established modern education. Education was viewed as a means for enhancing economic development, but in neither case were business leaders given much say in the key decisions relating to educational practice. For example, in Japan the Ministry of Education is responsible to the National Diet, so business leaders have to express their wishes through the political channel. At Japan's tertiary-level institutions, boards of trustees (on which business leaders often sit) run private universities, but there are no boards of directors in public sector universities. In the United States, business leaders may sit on the boards of school districts as well as on the boards of universities. However, it is generally regarded that business leaders have relatively little influence on the everyday decisions of American schools and universities. The relatively modest influence of the business sector has resulted in educational approaches that have few direct connections with the business world. Indeed, such benefits seem, if anything, to have declined over time. For example, the technical training aspects of the school system have decreased and, in recent years, are offered to only a small minority of all young people.

While business influence on the day-to-day decisions of education is relatively weak in both societies, the Japanese business community pays relatively more attention to the direction of educational practice. For example, such nationwide business organizations as Keidanren and Nikkeiren periodically carry out their independent analyses of educational practice and publish their conclusions in high-profile white papers. Also, individual corporations enter into direct relations with many secondary schools and universities for the purpose of recruiting new staff. The U.S. business community is less active in both respects, though over the past decade there have been some changes. For example, in the 1980s many businesses began to develop "compacts" with particular schools or school districts designed to improve the managerial principles of these systems. And several leading businessmen have donated large sums of money to educational systems (mainly colleges and universities) to assist these institutions in their reforms. Such direct donations are less common in Japan.

Options for International Education

Given the inward nation-building bias of U.S. and Japanese education, neither tradition placed special emphasis on international education. Rather, attention to other nations and cultures tended to be a second-order priority to be worked into the intermediate and advanced levels of education and/or for select groups of students who might assume key roles in international negotiations. While key areas such as mathematics and national language were treated as essential subjects to be taught daily at every grade level, foreign languages and the study of other countries were treated as optional, to be taught as electives or through special programs that might take place during vacation breaks. Given the resistance to international education, those interested in its expansion found they had to experiment with a variety of approaches. Especially in the years following World War II, the international educators devised a number of promising programmatic options. These options can be compared, using the following criteria:

Balance. Possibly the most celebrated postwar international education initiative is the Fulbright Program, proposed by Senator William Fulbright in 1946 to promote "mutual understanding." A particular feature of this program has been to establish rough parity in the number of participants going to and from particular pairs of nations. This concern with parity has led many programs to seek an "exchange" of participants between partner sites; hence for some, the phrase "international exchange" is synonymous with international education. Other programs are more one-way in nature, particularly those between less-developed countries that require technical development and more-developed societies that can provide valuable training in key technical areas. One of the main reasons for the current concern with U.S.-Japan educational exchange is that the two nations are virtually equivalent in terms of development, yet the balance in terms of international education is so skewed. Over 45,000 Japanese study in U.S. colleges and universities, while barely 2,000 Americans are studying at the tertiary level in Japan.

International or Transnational. The main thrust in postwar programmatic thinking has been to foster greater understanding between peoples of different nations, usually focusing on particular bilateral relations. Thus, for example, the U.S. Fulbright program, which is possibly the most influential of all programs, is structured around a number of bilateral commissions that foster exchanges between pairs of nations. While this "international paradigm" has reigned for the past 50 years, today there is growing interest in an approach that focuses on issues and actors that crosscut national boundaries. Issues such as peace and conflict resolution, free trade, human rights, and environmental preservation capture much interest, and actors such as grassroots organizations, nongovernmental organizations and multinational corporations become more prominent. Whereas programs have traditionally been spoken of as advancing international education, there will be need in the future to give more attention to transnational education.

Overseas or Not. The general goal of international/transnational education is to increase awareness and understanding of other peoples and cultures. There is much debate on what is required in order to achieve this objective, and it may be that an overseas experience is not necessary to gain the intended impact. Much, for example, can be accomplished through well-planned instruction focusing on other cultures, and in recent years some institutions have been able to build international dialogue into such instruction using the Internet or satellite TV. Indeed, such virtual options deserve enthusiastic encouragement, but the final test of the acquired skills can only be accomplished through direct face-to-face encounters; so it is hoped that the virtual experiences will not become a substitute for real-life overseas experiences.

Skills and/or Experience. A critical issue in these experiences is the choice of language. English is widely taught throughout the world, so reliance on English is one option. But this may limit communication with those cultures where English is not the native language. Whether or not an overseas experience is included, there remains the question of primary focus for the international program. One option is to focus on specific technical skills such as language and business management, or artistic skills such as pottery. Another option is to focus on an in-depth cultural experience such as home-stay and/or an internship in a local firm.

Age. Related to a program's goal is the stage in individual development at which a program should begin. The most popular pattern up to World War II focused on mature individuals, who were either in college or of that age group. Some were older and went overseas to gain advanced technical skills or the opportunity to work in a world-famous scientific laboratory. A new pattern that emerged after the war was to focus on younger people in the expectation that the personal impact would be greater. Thus, high school exchanges have come to flourish, and language instruction at the high school level has been given a renewed emphasis. The most recent initiative has been to focus on even younger people, especially for language training and sometimes also for exchanges. For example, some primary schools devote themselves entirely to developing facility in a particular foreign language.

Length of Exposure. To achieve a reasonable impact, it once was thought that a program should last for at least a year; in the case of some advanced programs, several years seemed appropriate. But the longer a program, the greater its cost and the smaller the number of people who are able to sacrifice the time. For these reasons, short-term programs have become increasingly popular.

While thinking in international education often focuses on particular programs, the concept of Transnational Competence encourages thinking about combinations of individual programs that stretch over a long period of time, each adding new strengths to prior accomplishments. **TNC involves lifelong education** in contrast to many contemporary approaches, which focus on discrete and often disconnected experiences.

After-Care. Most programs select individuals, get them to the program site, and spend some time taking care of individual needs while at the site. But after the individual completes the program, what next? Most programs simply return the individuals to their place of origin. However, some programs select adults in mid-career, thus interrupting their normal working routine. The goal of the program is to add an overseas dimension to the individual's work routine. But this goal can only be accomplished if the individual is able to return to a work setting that requires the overseas dimension. Sponsoring organizations sometimes offer to help the individuals find the appropriate setting.

Sectors and Sponsors. Essentially four groups have been involved in promoting and/or stand to benefit from international education programs: national governments, universities, corporations, and local communities or community-based organizations (e.g., Rotary International). In most instances, the sectors have created programs for their own benefit. Programs sponsored by communities have tended to send youth or community leaders to sister cities or counterpart community organizations in other countries, and universities have sent students or faculty to institutions where they have an exchange group. So the main direction of flow is between counterparts. The main exception is government, which has tended to support programs for all sectors.

Postwar Traditions of International Education in the United States

While international education has not achieved as firm a place as mathematics or science, it has been the focus of much creative thinking. In this and the next section, we review several of the key innovations.

Individual Cultivation. Through much of the 19th century, America viewed itself as a child of Europe, and this was reflected in educational curriculum at all levels, as well as the inclination of elites and scientists to follow European intellectual leaders. Foreign languages were essential components of both

the secondary and collegiate curriculum well into the 20th century, and educated people were inclined to spend some time in Europe on the "grand tour"
in order to broaden their horizons. On these tours, they visited the major
sites of culture and civilization, took in the major events, met the right people,
and improved their communication skills in the approved foreign languages.
The autobiographies of American elites such as Thomas Jefferson and Henry
James recount these experiences. As American education became more in-
stitutionalized, the concept of the grand tour was assimilated in the "mutual
understanding" tradition to be discussed below.

Grand tours were typically organized by individuals, in contrast to the more
formalized programs that were to follow. The unexpected outbreak of the
First World War enabled Americans to appreciate that there were complexities in international affairs far beyond their understanding. In response, some
foundations began to support modest programs of international education
resulting in, for example, the creation of the Institute of International Education (IIE) in 1919. In the late 1930s, to counter the influence of Germany and
Italy, the U.S. government announced the Convention for the Promotion of
Inter-American Cultural Relations, its first formal program in educational exchange. From the late 1800s through the Second World War, American mis-
sionaries were active in educational exchange, providing support for the establishment of foreign schools and universities and inviting foreign students
to study in the United States. But all in all, in the United States, international
education was a limited activity through World War II.

Table 2.2. Rationales and Beneficiaries of Major U.S. Programs

Rationale	Period	Beneficiaries
Individual Cultivation	Enduring	Individual, University
Mutual Understanding	1940s-1960s	Individual, Community, University, Nation, Humanity
Technical Advancement	1950s-1980s	Nation, University, Industry
National Security	1960s-1980s	Nation, Industry, University
Scientific Advancement	Periodic	Humanity, Nation, University, Industry
Competitiveness	1980s-now	Industry, Nation
Grassroots	1990s	Community, Humanity
Regional Order	1990s	Individual, Nation, Humanity

With the emergence of the United States as a world leader after World War
II, this situation changed dramatically. A great variety of new programs were
devised in keeping with America's new international responsibilities. Table
2.2 provides a listing of the main rationales for these programs, analyzed in

terms of the period of their genesis and the communities they purport to benefit. These postwar programs, on balance, were designed primarily to bring more people to the United States, rather than to increase the exposure of Americans to other places. In the following sections, we summarize several of the more salient features of the leading American programs, particularly as they relate to U.S.-Japan exchange.

Mutual Understanding. Many who experienced the first World War felt that it had been caused by a breakdown of communication between the different peoples of Europe. Thus, parallel with the establishment of the League of Nations, a number of student exchange programs were established to increase the international-mindedness of young people. The basic assumption of these programs was that the individuals who participated would acquire by their cross-cultural exposure a broader understanding and greater respect for both their own and other cultures. Additionally, it was assumed that the foreign visitors would add a new viewpoint to the campuses they visited and, in that way, enhance the quality of those environments.

While most of the above programs were unidirectional, involving either a desire by individuals of one culture to learn about another culture or a concern by a society to familiarize foreigners with their national situation, following World War II the United States introduced a new program which emphasized the principle of mutuality. In the words of the program's founder, Senator Fulbright:

> I believe that man's struggle to be rational about himself, about his
> relationship to his own society and to other peoples and nations
> involves a constant search for understanding among all peoples
> and all cultures - a search that can only be effective when learning
> is pursued on a world-wide basis. The educational exchange
> program is built on this premise which, stated another way, holds
> that America has much to teach the world but also much to learn,
> and that the greater our intellectual involvement with the world
> beyond our frontiers, the greater the gain for both America and the
> world (Johnson and Colligan, 1965, p.vii).

The original Fulbright program obtained funds from the debts owed to the United States under the lend-lease program and other wartime credits. In American and in numerous countries around the world, bilateral commissions were established to select outstanding local people who could benefit from studying, carrying out research, or teaching in the opposite country. From the beginning, the Fulbright program had an elitist character. The commissions sought to select future leaders and to place them in suitable institutions.

During the Kennedy era, two new departures within the mutual understanding tradition were the Peace Corps and the East-West Center. The former was an extension of the technical assistance theme to be described below, but relied on young Americans to provide assistance. Under this program, more than 10,000 young Americans spent two or more years in Asia, often in direct daily contact with local people. The program had a profound impact on the worldview of these young people. In contrast, the East-West Center was established in Hawaii as a special institution for promoting "technical and cultural exchange" between Asia, the Pacific, and the United States.

Over the postwar period, an increasing number of programs concerned with promoting cross-cultural understanding have adopted the principle of mutuality. At the collegiate level a popular approach is the junior-year-abroad program, often established through a reciprocal arrangement between two schools in two countries. As these reciprocal arrangements have multiplied, an ever-broader sector of American higher education has come both to receive foreign students and send Americans abroad. Goodwin and Nacht (1988) indicate that such programs, as well as the number of Americans participating in them, expanded rapidly over the 1980s. By the mid-1990s there were more than 500 agreements between American and Japanese universities, which at least on paper allowed the exchange of small numbers of students between the partner institutions.

Parallel to the growth of study-abroad programs have been a number of youth exchange programs established through a combination of public and community funds. Organizations such as Youth for Understanding and the American Field Service have emerged to coordinate these programs. They typically place young Americans in foreign settings for two to three months with local parents providing home-stays. In exchange, foreign families send their children to the United States, often for a full school year. The youth exchange programs began in the 1950s and were re-energized in the Reagan era.

Technical Assistance. As postwar relations became polarized in the Cold War and the United States witnessed the fury of Communist-inspired revolution in China and insurrection in Greece and Turkey, strategic planning broadened. Peace and freedom, it was argued, would depend on worldwide development, and the United States, as the richest and technologically most advanced society, would have to take the lead in establishing the conditions for this development. This new argument was boldly announced in President Harry Truman's inaugural address, where after affirming his commitment to supporting the United Nations, world economic recovery, and the need to "strengthen freedom-loving nations against the dangers of aggression," he added:

Fourth, we must embark on a bold new program for making the

benefits of our scientific advances and industrial progress available for the improvement and growth of underdeveloped areas.

This position led in 1950 to the passage of the Act for International Development and the establishment of what widely came to be known as America's Point Four Program of technical assistance. The Agency for Overseas Development (now USAID), attached to the State Department, became the implementing body.

For many of its projects, USAID defined the objective and then negotiated a contract for its implementation with an American university, usually of the land-grant group. These contracts included provisions for new technology, field consultants to manage the technology's introduction, and participant training so that key practitioners from the receiving society could acquire the skills and knowledge essential for using the technology.

Japan has never been a focus of USAID programs, but in the immediate postwar period the U.S.-led Occupation government created Government and Relief in Occupied Areas (GARIOA), which enabled several thousand Japanese, many who were assistants or faculty at universities and colleges, to pursue research and advanced education in the United States.

Foundations and Technical Assistance. Concurrent with the inauguration of Point Four was the decision by America's foundations to address the problem of Third World development. The foundations sought to provide the cutting edge in development work. While having less money, a few internationally oriented foundations were inclined to assume they had more wisdom than the U.S. government and, for that matter, than the countries they were seeking to help. Thus, the foundations were not hesitant to propose and implement their own remedies.

National Security. In the Cold War era, especially prominent has been the desire to establish effective arrangements with strategic allies around the world so as to guarantee international political stability. One important element in this strategy has been the negotiation of military assistance agreements with various foreign governments. In the immediate postwar period, military assistance was a small fraction of technical assistance, but it has expanded rapidly to the point where it currently constitutes two-fifths of all foreign assistance.

Military assistance agreements typically involve both the provision of military hardware and the training required to make effective use of the hardware. Much of this training occurs at U.S. military installations while some, especially that dealing with more theoretical and contextual questions, is subcontracted to American universities and corporations. More foreigners have come to the United States under military assistance than under any other program.

Complementing the policy of providing allies with advanced military techniques is a second element, that of obtaining information about potentially troublesome international situations and interpreting this information. The American foundations were among the first to articulate this necessity. A report to the Ford Foundation by Richard Spaeth argued that "one of the first things the Foundation should do is to train, to devise ways to build up more competence in the United States about those areas in the postwar world we have to relate to in one way or another." As this argument was eventually developed, it proposed that the universities would be the ideal location for developing those wise experts with special knowledge of isolated countries. In the wake of Sputnik, these ideas coalesced in 1958 in the National Defense Education Act (NDEA), whose purpose was to "ensure trained manpower of sufficient quality and quantity to meet the national defense needs of the United States." Along with science and mathematics, foreign languages were among the areas in which training was to be supported. Thus was born the foreign language and area studies fellowship program.

The substantial funds authorized in this legislation were used to establish numerous area studies centers across the country and provide fellowships eventually for more than 20,000 students. While the student fellowships under this program were limited to American citizens, center funds could be used for inviting foreign researchers. Many centers found other donors, especially foundations, willing to supplement the government funds, thus enabling varied and rich programs. Over time, the United States became the world center for the study of many parts of the world.

But problems gradually emerged in this wedding of national security interests with the missions of the autonomous universities. Beginning in the mid-1960s, as the universities became the base for critical analysis of America's policies in Southeast Asia, government and Congressional critics began to re-examine the premise of NDEA.

Meanwhile, a glut of area specialists began to appear in the labor market due to a combination of saturation of area specialist positions in the major universities and an oversupply of new scholars. While some graduates found employment in government and other places, many remained unemployed (Lambert, 1973; McDonnell, 1983).

The combination of declining government interest and low employability created major morale problems for those involved in the study of foreign cultures. The number of applicants to the area studies centers has since declined, and as one recent study puts it, America is searching for a new equilibrium "beyond growth."

While area studies at the major universities has leveled off, many lesser universities and colleges have established small programs, and the number of students going overseas under the NDEA (now National Research Center) program and other related programs is still quite substantial. But it is still unclear whether the national capacity to understand and deal effectively with foreign societies is as sharp as it was in the mid-1960s golden age of area studies.

Scientific Progress. Less celebrated than some of the traditions discussed above but more enduring is the tradition of going overseas in the pursuit of universal truths, as embodied in the scientific tradition. The quest for scientific knowledge is relatively indifferent to national boundaries or interests. Throughout the early decades of the 20th century, leading American scholars took it for granted that they should visit Europe to discover recent trends in their fields. As American institutions became better endowed and the level of American scientific inquiry improved, European scholars in increasing numbers began to visit American institutions. During and after the Second World War, with European universities in chaos, many European scientists moved permanently to the United States to take up positions in American institutions. Over the postwar period, American universities have sought to identify the best scholars regardless of nationality, attracting many foreign experts to the United States.

While individual scholars and their institutions once provided the major source of funds for the pursuit of scientific knowledge, after World War II the U.S. Congress, recognizing the close relation between scientific progress and the prosperity of the American people, authorized the National Science Foundation (NSF) as a permanent federal agency to promote scientific inquiry in the natural sciences and engineering. At the same time, a number of standing agencies were consolidated in the National Institute of Health (NIH) to focus on the biological sciences and health. Over time the budgets of these agencies have vastly increased, as have the budgets of a number of large scientific laboratories established on the recommendation of the NSF, including Argonne, Oak Ridge, and Woods Hole. In pursuit of the scientific objectives outlined in the various projects funded by NSF and other such bodies, large numbers of scientists and apprentice scientists are involved, including quite a few from Japan (National Science Board, 1983, p.30).

Apart from project-related recruitment, NSF also has developed a fellowship program to support graduate study as well as other programs to support short- and long-term visitations by scholars at research sites. Many of these grants take Americans overseas and bring foreign scientists to the United States. In recent years, recognizing the advantages of sustained exchanges with scientists in Japan and other places, NSF has negotiated a number of bilateral agreements to increase the interaction with these areas.

Science in the view of NSF is primarily natural science and engineering. While NSF supports some social science research, a number of other bodies are also established for this purpose, including the National Institutes of Health, the Social Science Research Council, and the National Institute of Education. The first two bodies in particular have sizeable programs for the support of overseas study.

Competitive Business. During the immediate postwar period, the United States was the world's leader in industrial productivity and international trade. In virtually every respect, the American economy dominated in international transactions. In subsequent decades, America has continued to demonstrate leadership in technical innovation and has moved increasing shares of its capital overseas to take advantage of low foreign wages. Partly for this reason, America's edge in international trade has declined.

In the mid-1970s, American leaders began to evidence concern about their declining trade position, especially in Asia, the world's most rapidly growing market. Japan and other newly industrializing countries were outselling in product areas and markets where America had traditionally dominated. In part, the American decline could be attributed to the high cost of American products. However, according to some business leaders, a second factor was the lack of an effective American presence in many markets. America did not have as many businessmen overseas as did her major competitors, and those who were overseas did not have the language and cultural skills required for carrying out business in Asia.

This perception of an inadequate American presence has energized some business and law schools to develop joint programs that include an area studies component. It has also led to new programs for sending Americans overseas to study foreign languages and customs while in professional schools or prior to entry. The Engineering Alliance for Global Education (EAGLE) is a promising consortium that has enabled upwards of 200 U.S. engineering students and over 75 interns to gain experience in Japan. In addition, some American corporations have developed programs to bring foreigners to the United States (Zikopoulos and Barber, 1984). One weakness in some of these programs is that the participants have difficulty, after completion of their programs, in finding jobs. Partly in response to this problem, the U.S. Department of Commerce has developed the Manufacturing Technology Program for in-career corporate researchers who, with the support of their companies, are provided language study and internships in Japanese laboratories. Commerce, in collaboration with Japan's Ministry of International Trade and Industry, is able to find interesting spots in a wide variety of Japanese corporate laboratories for these interns.

Key Issues in U.S. International Education

Reviewing the several American traditions, we find from the late 1940s a progressive involvement of the federal government in the sponsorship of international education as the rationales of mutual understanding, national security and competitiveness were added to the long-standing concerns for individual cultivation, scientific advancement, and technical and cultural influence. The various postwar programs had a peculiar influence on the capacity of the U.S. to cultivate Transnational Competence, which we review below.

The Faith in Higher Education. In large part because university leaders were consulted in the development of these various programs, most of the postwar American programs have tended to contribute to the internationalization of higher education. The Fulbright program has enabled American scholars and students to travel to other countries and has brought outstanding scholars and students (usually at the graduate level) to American campuses. USAID's sponsorship of technical assistance led to large contracts for a number of American universities, enabling them to establish offices for international programs to carry out these off-site activities. The Higher Education Act and other related legislation, in conjunction with the support of foundations, enabled a number of universities to develop area studies. The President's Commission on Foreign Language Studies of 1978-79, in which Senator Paul Simon played a key role, gave impetus to the activities to strengthen foreign language and area studies. More recently, many universities have been subsidized in the development of programs in international business and management. Whereas international education was often an inconspicuous component of prewar campuses, by the mid-1980s every university in the Association of American Universities (AAU) had an office of international programs.

The introduction of area studies was accompanied by a significant diversification of the languages offered at American universities and colleges. Whereas European languages dominated the scene, increasing numbers of institutions added Asian and African languages. Japanese became increasingly popular over the 1980s, and once again between 1990 and 1995 the numbers of collegiate-level students enrolled in Japanese doubled. Chinese also has increased in popularity.

Yet while foreign language study became more diverse, many institutions eliminated the requirement of two years of foreign language as a prerequisite for graduation. So while Asian foreign languages have experienced gains, total enrollments in foreign languages have actually stabilized. The study of a foreign language is an important recruiting ground for study abroad, so the relaxation of foreign language requirements may have had a negative impact on the level of participation in these programs.

Yet another dimension of "international" expansion was the influx of foreign students, from less than 50,000 in the mid-1950s to more than 400,000 by the mid-1990s. In the sciences and engineering, many of these students stayed on to take positions as postdoctoral researchers and as faculty members, thus further contributing to the internationalization of American higher education.

In sum, the impact of America's postwar international education boom on higher education has been profound.

The Neglect of School Education. In contrast with the international education boom's impressive impact on higher education, it seems to have had very little impact on secondary school education. For example, at the turn of the century the American educational system still retained many of the features of classical European education, including significant coverage of world (i.e., European) history as well as the study of two foreign languages; in many schools, the required languages were Greek and Latin.

Over the next several decades secondary education expanded dramatically, and by the time of World War II had come to include three of every four young Americans of the appropriate age. Foreign language study, while generally required, shifted to modern languages. Up to World War I, German was the most popular language, but then French, Italian, and later Spanish increased in popularity. Apart from in Hawaii, which was still a territory, Asian languages were not featured in the school curriculum. The important point is that every high school student was expected to study a foreign language. But the rapid expansion of secondary education that began in the 1930s, resulting in the inclusion of most American young people, led educators to question the appropriateness of requiring all students to follow an identical curriculum. More and more schools came to make certain subjects elective, especially foreign languages. Thus the proportion of young people taking foreign languages declined.

The trend of declining enrollments continued through the mid-1980s at which time less than a quarter of American high school students took more than two years of a foreign language. In sum, during the same period that higher education was benefiting from the international education boom, foreign language education at the pre-collegel level was in retreat. Only after the mid-1980s did secondary school foreign language enrollment begin to head upwards again, but even so, by the mid-1990s only one-third of all high school students were taking a foreign language.

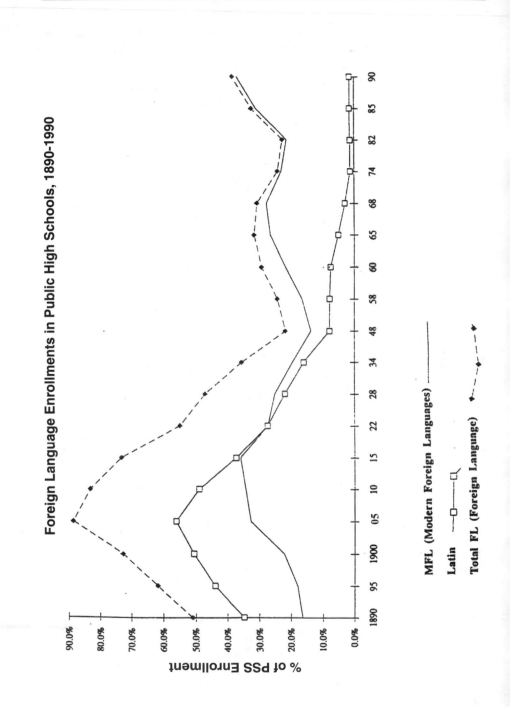

Foreign Language Enrollments in Public High Schools, 1890-1990

Source: Draper, Jamie. 1991. Foreign language enrollments in public secondary schools, fall 1989
1990. American Council on the Teaching of Foreign Languages: Yonkers, NY ERIC, Ed. 340 214 1.

Of those at the school level studying foreign languages, Spanish became by far the most popular. Asian languages were introduced into a number of schools, particularly in Hawaii and on the West Coast, but Asian languages were still a minority choice compared to Spanish. By the early 1990s, for example, only about 42,000 American high school students were receiving formal instruction in Japanese. This is about one-half of the number who later in college decided to study Japanese or other matters relating to Japan. While in the case of European languages and culture, far more young people receive exposure in high school than elect to follow up in college, the reverse is the case for Japan.

Insofar as tertiary-level transnational learning experiences depend on facility in a foreign language, **it is apparent that America's high schools do not provide American young people with an adequate foundation.** Those at the collegiate level who seek a transnational experience have to weigh the advantages of such programs against the disadvantage of having to devote precious time to introductory language study.

The lack of advances in school-level foreign language education is only one indication of the way schools have been shortchanged. While college professors have access to a wide variety of programs for going abroad to spend a sabbatical teaching or doing research, there are fewer programs for school-teachers; in the later stages of the National Defense Education Act, school outreach was added as a condition for a university accepting a grant, but few universities gave high priority to these activities. Also, there have been few global or international secondary education initiatives sponsored by foundations or government agencies over the past several decades, in contrast with the host of programs sponsored for colleges and universities. In sum, the international education programs of America's secondary schools have been sadly neglected. Despite the renewed educational rhetoric at the national level, international education is not included in the list of Goals for 2000, nor was international education highlighted in President Clinton's 1997 State of the Union Address, an address focused largely on the challenges facing American education.

The Impact on the Government and Corporate Sectors. Over the past two decades, there has been increasing interest in programs that have direct benefits for the government and corporate sectors, but it is not clear that major success has been achieved in this regard.

The programs that focus on national security have led to a considerable development of knowledge about various parts of the world not formerly accessible in the United States. While much of this knowledge was produced in universities, some government agencies also have developed new capabilities in international work, notably in such areas as defense, intelligence, diplomacy, and lately in commerce and trade. But over the past decade, re-duced levels of government recruitment have limited the ability of government agencies to enhance their international capabilities.

Top corporate executives express considerable interest in programs that provide them with new recruits who combine good business skills with a grasp of foreign markets (including experience and language skills). But at the stage of recruiting new employees, graduates from these programs are viewed with considerable skepticism by corporations. Corporations are especially reluctant to participate in those programs that offer mid-career overseas opportunities to their employees. So despite the rhetoric of national security and competitiveness, there remain weaknesses in the way some recent programs are performing.

Immigration Versus International Education. One reason why U.S. corporations do not evidence great interest in programs designed to develop young people's business and cultural skills is that the corporations have other means to recruit such people. Thanks to the large numbers of foreign students in the United States, if an American-based corporation seeks to place someone in China or Indonesia, there is a reasonable chance that they can locate a native of that country who has received business or technical training in the United States. The corporation has the option of either hiring the individual as a local employee in the target country or hiring him/her as a U.S. appointee and taking out residency papers. In the corporation's view, the individual with a local background may stand a better chance of coping with the local challenges than an American citizen who has only a partial command of the relevant foreign language and culture. This example points out an interesting conflict between America's attempt to internationalize Americans and America's enthusiasm for welcoming foreign students. In some instances, these two impulses work at cross-purposes.

The Ideology/Support Gap. With the passing of the Cold War, the responsibility of the federal government for international education is less clear, for the major initiatives supported by the federal government focus on Cold War issues of mutual understanding, national security and technical assistance. Thus over the last several years, federal commitment to international education has waned. Programs such as USAID and United States Information Agency (USIA) (including Fulbright) have experienced large cutbacks. The emerging ideologies of competitiveness, regional order, and grassroots involvement imply that the future beneficiaries of international/transnational education are more likely to be local communities and large corporations than the nation as a whole. Yet at least in the case of the United States, these prospective beneficiaries are not prepared to provide resources to support new programs. It can be said that international/transnational education in the

United States is facing a funding crisis.

Japan's Traditions of International Education

The Japanese traditions of international education have conceptual parallels to the American concepts. However, the Japanese traditions are more closely associated with national goals, and perhaps for this reason the Japanese traditions seem more purposeful. Also, because of Japan's deeper interest in international education, international themes as well as foreign language preparation are more evident in the formal educational system. For those reasons, Japanese young people have a more solid foundation in international education than do young Americans. Moreover, in recent years Japanese enthusiasm for international education has begun to accelerate at the very time that interest in the United States is subsiding.

Ryugakusei. Japan has a longer history than the United States, and overseas study there has a more extended tradition. The first great wave of international education occurred in the 6th century when large numbers of young Japanese became intrigued with the wisdom of Buddhism and traveled to China to learn more; over the next two centuries as these students came back and put their knowledge to practice, Japan's institutions were significantly transformed. During this period, the concept of ryugakusei was developed, which can be translated as an individual who travels in search of knowledge.[9] The students of that period were purposeful and tended to devote several years to their overseas investigations, and as they were seeking foreign knowledge they always had to achieve mastery of a foreign language. Later episodes of overseas study have tended to be influenced by and modeled on this first wave of experience.

Enlightenment and/or National Security. Japan's second great wave of international education began with the Meiji Restoration, when the new leaders declared the nation "should seek knowledge throughout the world."[10] Several thousand young Japanese were sponsored to go overseas and learn various aspects of western technology and civilization. Most were sent by

---

[9] In the Meiji period, the term became kaigai ryugaku to cover various types of overseas travel for study. The government made a distinction between ryugakusei for extended study and shisatsusha (observers) for more casual study (see Conte, 1976).

[10] In fact, a number of students were sent by the shogunate and certain fiefs prior to the Restoration. For example, Arinori Mori, who was later to play a key role in the development of the modern Japanese educational system, was sent to England in 1865 by the Lord of Satsuma. (Bennett et al., 1958, p. 30). In 1871, some 250 were selected and sent by the soon-to-be-abolished feudal lords on the instruction of the recently constituted Meiji government, though a year later most were recalled (Schwantes, 1955, pp. 194-195).

the central government, with local governments also sometimes serving as sponsors. The Meiji Emperor in 1871 observed:

> After careful study and observation, I am deeply impressed with the belief that the most powerful and enlightened nations of the world are those who have made diligent effort to cultivate their minds, and sought to develop their country in the fullest and most perfect manner.... If we would profit by the useful arts and sciences and conditions of society prevailing among more enlightened nations, we must either study these at home as best we can, or send abroad an expedition of practical observers to foreign lands, competent to acquire for us those things our people lack, which are best calculated to benefit this nation (Lanman, 1931, pp. 2-3).

Among the more celebrated official missions was that of Prince Iwakura from 1871 to 1872 to investigate various institutions in Europe and the United States. On their return, the members of this mission began to draft regulations for the new Japan. Among these was the Gakusei (Educational System), outlining the basic framework for Japan's modern educational system, which was to be centralized with a predominantly western curriculum.

In the first years of the Meiji period, most overseas study was ad hoc in response to suddenly discerned needs for new insights or knowledge. But in 1875, the government issued a set of regulations seeking to formalize the procedures both for defining objectives and selecting future candidates for official overseas study. From that time, the number going annually under government sponsorship tended to stabilize at about 150 per year.

In the early years, Japan's overseas students tended to be spread equally among various destinations. But by the mid-Meiji period a view had developed in Japan that Europe, and particularly Germany, was the best place for academic study, especially in such fields as science, medicine, and the humanities. America was seen as more advantageous for new fields such as business and accounting or the applied sciences. In the early years of the Meiji period, most officially sponsored ryugakusei entered specialized programs or studies toward a bachelor degree. As Japan's modern educational system strengthened, most stayed in Japan to complete their bachelor's degree, and then proceeded overseas for more advanced study. Increasingly those going overseas were destined for careers in academia, studying for the purpose of advancing science.

Over time, there emerged a tendency of merit selection to replace the former tendency of patronage. It is said that the quality and level of preparation of candidates sharply improved. Most of those chosen for study either had an official position prior to their departure, or had reason to expect such a position on their return. **It is difficult to find in the United States a parallel to Japan's practice of sending promising young civil servants for in-career assignments of overseas study.** The practice continues to the present day, and especially in recent years has also been actively imitated by Japanese corporations, which send large numbers of promising young employees for courses in foreign business schools.

Scientific Advancement/Cooperation. "Western Science and Eastern Spirit" was one of the more prominent of the many slogans proclaimed at the dawn of the Meiji era. Large sums were expended to invite western technicians and scientists to teach eager Japanese students at such institutions as the Kobusho and Tokyo University, later to become the Imperial University. And many of the young people sent overseas were expected to specialize in scientific fields. To expedite the success of these overseas study tours, both science and foreign languages were stressed in the schools; at the more advanced educational institutions, foreign professors were encouraged to lecture in their native languages.

By the mid-Meiji period Japan had developed a core of scientists who were proficient in foreign languages and able to follow the latest scientific developments. Of course, given Japan's position as a late developer, the indigenous definition of science was somewhat broader than in the West. For example, when the Imperial University was founded in 1886, alongside the Faculty of Natural Science were also the more applied Faculties of Medicine and Engineering; only five years later the Faculty of Agriculture was added. Science was viewed more as a tool for development than as an endeavor for pursuing fundamental discoveries. It was not until the Taisho period (the second decade of the 20th century) that Japanese science began to distinguish itself in international scientific circles. To assist Japanese scientists in these pragmatic efforts, considerable funds were made available to acquire foreign publications and to translate these into Japanese. Also, special funds were created to invite leading foreign scientists to visit Japan and give special lectures.

The Ministry of Education was the principal agency in charge of promoting Japan's scientific advancement. As early as 1875 a special bureau for Higher Education and Science was established, and one mission of this bureau was to coordinate the overseas trips of Japanese scholars and invite leading foreign scholars to Japan.

Needless to say, scholarly exchange slowed during the Second World War, and following the war the Occupation carefully monitored the travel of scholars. Japanese scientists were not allowed to go abroad until 1948, and given the strong presence of Americans in the Occupation government, the major direction of travel was to the United States. This began what one observer describes as the Americanization of Japanese science, as contrasted with the prewar European orientation.

Following the Occupation, the Ministry reinstated its own programs for scholarly exchange. The Japan Society for the Promotion of Science, formally established in 1957, is the organization now performing most of these scholarly exchange functions on behalf of the Ministry of Education and Culture. At the same time, the Ministry has separate funds to send scholars affiliated with national universities overseas as well as to invite research scholars to spend time at selected universities and research centers.

In recent years, several other government agencies have developed programs to encourage foreign researchers to visit Japan for varying lengths of time. For example, many of the innovative grants from the Science and Technology Agency encourage the inclusion of foreign researchers in project research groups.

Cultural Diplomacy. Due to the long period of forced isolation prior to the Meiji Restoration, Japan is keenly conscious both of its affinity with other nations, and its uniqueness. In the early stages of modernization, the national government was concerned with building good will internationally so as to forestall the imperial interests of western powers. Thus, considerable funds were allocated for inviting foreign visitors to Japan and for sending Japanese cultural emissaries abroad. This practice abated after World War II due to the new austerity.

But in the early 1970s Japan experienced the famous Nixon shock when the United States negotiated a one-China agreement without first advising Japan of its plans. Japan's leaders concluded that foreign nations did not understand the special concerns of Japan, and something had to be done. One result was the establishment of the Japan Foundation as a quasi-governmental agency for promoting better understanding of Japan abroad. Much of the early activities of the Japan Foundation were focused on the United States, promoting Japanese studies there and the expansion of Japanese language training in U.S. colleges and high schools.

Subsequently, the Japan Foundation has increased its scope to Europe, Asia, and other parts of the world. Particularly in Asia, the Japan Foundation has focused on cultivating a sense of cultural affinity. Hajime Nakamura, a prominent Japanese philosopher, in speaking to a group of Asian intellectuals invited to Japan by the Japan Foundation, once cited the noted art critic Tenshin Okakura's (1863-1913) assertion that "Asia is One" (Nakamura, 1980, p. 5). The Foundation has established Japan Chairs in various Asian universities and supported the restoration of various archeological treasures. In addition, many Asian scholars have been supported for study in Japan.

Individual Advancement. Distinct from government-sponsored students were many others who, recognizing the career value of overseas study, decided to set out on their own or with private sponsorship. Christian missions seeking to gain influence in Japan were responsible for some of these students, such as Jo Nijima, who upon his return to Japan set about founding a school that later became Doshisha University. Many others, however, simply set out on their own with no form of sponsorship. By the turn of the 20th century, these independent overseas students outnumbered the official students, especially among those going to America.

Mixed in with those seeking to use overseas study to advance bureaucratic and business careers was a growing minority who traveled to the West to study art, music, and other aesthetic traditions.

Just as in the case of officially supported scholars, these independent students evidenced impressive commitment to overseas study. Most sought to fit in with the demands of their overseas environment, mastering foreign languages and accepting foreign foods and customs. The typical ryugakusei stayed in his (or her) foreign locale for a minimum of a year and more typically for several years. Among the ryugakusei, those who entered an academic course such as a bachelor's degree program usually intended to complete the course, not just gain a taste.

While government-sponsored students could expect to return to an official post, the independent students often had no clear future ahead of them. The absence of a clear future is said to have enabled this group to be more experimental, and thus many acquired more liberal social and political dispositions. This was expressed in their relative freedom in striking up friendships overseas and, perhaps most importantly, in their more iconoclastic tendencies on their return. For example, independent students were more likely to identify with liberal political groups, and contributed to the steady opening of Japanese society.

The volume of independent students slowed to a trickle in the late 1930s, but picked up again in the late 1960s. Especially from the mid-1980s, as the yen increased in value, this tradition became more prominent. At least eight of every ten Japanese students currently in the United States are there for individual advancement. Many of these are young women taking non-degree ESL courses.

Technical Assistance. Up to World War II, there were few intergovernmental arrangements for overseas study. However, following the war the Japanese government had little money to spare, and thus the offer by the U.S. government to sponsor selected Japanese students for U.S. study under the GARIOA program (Government and Relief in Occupied Areas) was welcomed.

For several years, this was the major avenue for Japanese citizens to study overseas, superceded by the 1952 launching of the Japan-U.S. Fulbright exchanges which have grown into one of the largest bilateral Fulbright programs in the world, with substantial Japanese public and private funding supplementing the U.S. government contribution.

During this same period, Japan completed the various negotiations associated with concluding World War II. A major outcome of these negotiations was the requirement that Japan provide reparations to various Asian governments (both in payments and services). One of the services that Japan came to provide was the opportunity for Asian students to study in Japan. Within a few years of receiving technical assistance from the United States, Japan began to provide such assistance to other nations.

In the mid-1970s, Japan enlarged the concept of technical assistance with a formal program of Overseas Development Assistance. Initially the focus of ODA was on large construction projects, but as time has passed the allocations for training have increased. These funds have brought many people from developing countries to Japan for training at various levels, including industry and formal educational institutions, especially the higher technical schools and universities. Currently upwards of 40,000 trainees and 10,000 students are in Japan with ODA funding.

Internationalization. By the early 1980s Japan was viewed as a major power, particularly in the economic arena. Japan's trade balance with virtually every major country in the world was consistently in the black, and Japanese prowess in efficient management and the production of high-quality products was achieving recognition. Yet Japan was beginning to ask whether, if left alone, it could keep up the momentum.

At about this time, Yasuhiro Nakasone was elected Prime Minister, and he decided to promote a new policy of "internationalization" as part of his plan to restructure Japan's external relations. This idea was debated in various circles, including the Prime Minister's Special Council for Educational Reform (Rinkyoshin), leading to the conclusion that internationalization would enable Japan to be more creative in its intellectual life (if foreign researchers were to work alongside Japanese nationals) and more competitive in its commercial life (if both Japanese and foreign nationals found it easier to go back and forth between Japan and other destinations).

This new policy was infused in various sectors, but perhaps its biggest impact was in education, where new high schools were established to make it easier for the children of overseas Japanese to return to Japan, and universities were urged to radically expand their intake of foreign students. Indeed, in a 1984 policy statement Prime Minister Nakasone proposed that the number of foreign students in Japan would be increased from the circa 10,000 of that time to 100,000 by the year 2000. Another important innovation at the high school level was the JET program, which has invited many (over 3,000 in 1996) native English-speakers to assist Japanese instructors in English language instruction. The value of this program for Japanese high school students is yet to be assessed, but it is clear that the year (or two) of living in Japan had a profound impact on the aspirations and interests of the numerous foreigners sponsored by the JET program. Parallel to the JET program, a smaller number of Japanese schoolteachers were sent to the United States and other countries to assist in Japanese language instruction and other subjects.

The "internationalization" policy has continued to provide the rationale for reforms down to the present, including the development of foreign-student dormitories, international student offices, the stimulation of new junior-year-abroad curricula and, most recently, the creation of many new scholarships for high school and college youth.

Regionalism. While the "internationalization" policy has had a western bias, many key people in Japan recognize that Japan's destiny is increasingly linked with the Asian region, where Japan has rich cultural ties and where an increasing proportion of Japanese investment and trade is directed. Thus, most of the above programs have included some consideration of Asia. For example, the great majority of overseas students in Japanese universities are from East Asia. And, as noted, the Japan Foundation has been particularly active in establishing Japan chairs in Asia.

However, particularly since the late 1980s, Japan has begun to search for new approaches to signify its commitment to Asia. One example is Japan's involvement in UMAP, a program to improve the linkage of universities in the Asian region. UMAP proposes to promote scholarly and student exchange between affiliated universities in the Asian region and gradually, through the establishment of degree equivalency and other means, to break down the barriers between the respective educational systems. Another example is a proposal recently floated by the Japanese Ministry of Foreign Affairs to establish a new Pacific Rim university in Okinawa. Asia regionalism is an emerging theme in the Japanese approach to international education that is destined to influence practice in the decades to come. But as will be stressed in Chapter Five of this report, the accomplishments to-date are woefully inadequate.

Grassroots Diplomacy. A final theme worthy of note is the recent Japanese interest in fostering nongovernmental or grassroots linkages through international education. It might, on the face of it, appear incongruous that Japan, the archetypal "developmental state," would be disposed to support grassroots activities. But Japan has always appreciated the role of local government in strengthening national solidarity. And in recent years Japan has developed an increasing appreciation for the contribution of nongovernmental organizations. A particularly noteworthy example was the speed and effectiveness of these organizations in responding to the challenge of the Kobe earthquake of 1995 at a time when the national government seemed indecisive.

A variety of channels has evolved to support grassroots linkages. Sister City linkages are one example, and in Japan these are quite numerous and active. Japanese organizations such as Rotary International also give high priority to international educational exchanges. The theme of grassroots linkages has from the mid-1980s also been given high priority by the Sasakawa Peace Foundation, one of Japan's largest private foundations with an international portfolio. And in 1991 the Japanese Ministry of Foreign Affairs created the Center for Global Partnership within the Japan Foundation as a vehicle for encouraging grassroots linkages, as well as expanding intellectual dialogues.

Key Issues in Japanese International Education

Japan has a strong commitment to international education. The sense of need can be traced to the Meiji Restoration, when Japan recognized it was hopelessly behind in modern technology and would have to learn so much in order to catch up. It also comes from the fact that Japan is a lonely country on the edge of Asia, but with a greater dependence on such nations as Saudi Arabia (for oil) and the United States (for export markets) than on her Asian neighbors. To do well, Japan has to be international.

Japan's commitment to international education begins with the school curriculum, which gives considerable attention to world history, and foreign culture and languages starting from the primary level. For example, western art and western music are featured in the art and music curricula of the elementary schools. And at the lower-secondary level, all Japanese young people are required to study English. At the upper-secondary level they are required to study at least one foreign language (almost always English).

While Japan's commitment and these strong foundations in the school curriculum are impressive, perhaps the biggest issue Japan faces today is the definition of internationalism. One aspect of this issue was debated extensively by the Prime Minister's Council on Educational Reform. In essence, **is internationalism primarily an activity to improve Japan's position in the world, or is internationalism an activity to improve the world?** While the Council leaned somewhat in the direction of the first position, there are many in Japan who respectfully differ.

A second issue is the scope of internationalism. While Japan devotes considerable resources to internationalism, these are heavily concentrated on Japan's traditional trading partners, who are the United States and Western Europe. Yet over the past decade Japan has significantly expanded its investment and trade with various Asian partners, notably Korea, Taiwan, China, and Thailand. And other nations, largely in Asia, are likely to increase their interaction with Japan. Yet Japanese internationalism does not reach out to these countries in the same way it reaches out to the West. A broadening of the geographic focus of what is international is another major challenge to Japan's approach to international education.

Distinct from the above is the raising of the fundamental question, What is Japan? Most of Japan's programs are predicated on the assumption that Japan is a monolithic nation, with a homogenous culture that should stay that way. But in recent decades, many Japanese are discovering their regional cultures and beginning to sense that what may be good for Japan may not be good for them. The shift from a monolithic nationalism to a diversified localism is a third challenge, partially expressed in the new interest in regionalism and grassroots initiatives.

At the same time, as Japan opens its doors to more and more foreigners for study, tourism, trade, and investment collaboration, new contacts are forged. The friendships that are formed lead increasing numbers of foreigners to participate in Japan, to educate their children in Japanese schools, to vote in Japanese elections, to seek a more complete acceptance in Japanese society. So a fourth challenge is for Japan to broaden its identity toward a multicultural and more inclusive focus.

Conclusion

Through much of the past century, Japan and the United States maintained respectful relations with each other, but there was little cultural interchange. Then suddenly the two nations were engaged in a bitter war. And soon after the war, the two nations found they needed each other to resist the threat of Asian communism. It was as if Japan and the United States were thrown together in a shotgun marriage. This checkered history of affiliation has provided a weak foundation for the very extensive interaction currently taking place between these two nations. While a level of understanding and trust has been established among key political and bureaucratic leaders, this is less so in the corporate world or in local communities. Of course, some areas of the United States, such as Hawaii and the West Coast, have stronger ties to certain areas of Japan, notably Hokkaido, the Tokyo area, and Okayama.

In the arena of culture and education, there is a significant imbalance in images and information. The Japanese media, school curricula and textbooks, and popular culture give far more attention to the United States than does American culture to Japan. Similarly, Japanese educators are more familiar with American education than vice versa. Indeed, many features of the Japanese educational structure have been modeled on the American precedent. University graduation in the two countries requires essentially the same number of "credit hours," and there is a similar balance between general and specialized subjects. These basic similarities bode well for reformers who seek to increase the level of educational interaction between the two countries. But beyond these similarities are important differences in the meaning of education and of overseas study that create big challenges. And there are also many practical difficulties such as differences in the administrative and academic calendars of the two systems. The chapters that follow will look more deeply into these similarities and differences.

Chapter Three

Basic Principles for Improving International Education

After examining current programs of international education, we developed eight principles for improvement, which are listed below (Table 3.1). It is our view that this list of improvements provides a useful standard for evaluating any program of international education. In this chapter, we introduce these principles and reflect on the special strengths and weaknesses of the U.S.-Japan experience. The discussion below will set the foundations for identifying in Chapters Four through Six the specific changes required for the new era of transnationalism.

Systematizing International Education

The previous chapter reminds us that international education, as practiced today, is the sum of a remarkable variety of discrete initiatives, each designed for a distinctive purpose and a special clientele. In the United States, leaders of colleges and universities have shown the greatest initiative while in Japan, the ministries in charge respectively of education and foreign affairs have been most prominent. As illustrated in Chapter Two, **most past initiatives have focused on elite and professional groups**, preparing them for specific roles as diplomats, scholars, intelligence officers, and so on. The elite and specialized focus of these programs has enabled them to develop largely as add-ons to the mainstream system of education, rather than as constituent parts. While add-on programs may be effective for the specialized and highly motivated elite clientele, they are less successful in reaching the larger group of citizens who need Transnational Competence and in transmitting the full range of skills required for TNC.

To both improve the quality of international education and expand its impact to a larger cross-section of the general public, we conclude that a more integrated systemic approach to international education is needed.

Table 3.1 Basic Principles for Improving International Education

Images should reflect realities

Encourage greater flow of popular culture

Seek better balance in news coverage

Challenge irresponsible journalism

Publicize technical and scientific accomplishments

Examine and publicize the value of overseas study

Information can become more accessible

Provide overseas study opportunities on Internet

Provide abstracts of overseas research on Internet

Provide information on funding opportunities

Increase the translation of high-quality cultural, technological, and scientific publications

Infrastructure should be built up and unnecessary barriers lowered

Back up information with effective placement consultation

Promote international student services, especially in Japan

Enable foreign nonprofit service organizations to operate more effectively

Simplify application requirements, procedures (e.g., visas, guarantee letters)

Improve vertical articulation

Between universities and schools

Between universities and regional cultural and business associations

Between the educational institutions that provide the experiences, the governments, and the NGOs that provide infrastructure

Between the universities and the employers that hire their graduates

Integration of key actors leads to greater impact

Stress strong and self-sustaining horizontal linkages:

Between high schools

Between universities

Between local communities and governments

Between corporations, especially to articulate their human resource needs

Improvements are urged in program quality

Foster multimedia virtual learning experiences

Strengthen the quality of study-abroad curricula (and create mechanisms for credit transfers)

Add study abroad as a realistic option in bachelor's level programs, including selected programs in law, engineering, business, and other professional areas

Improve and expand language instruction

In the United States, explore new avenues for high school Japanese language education

Require foreign language competency in all bachelor's degree programs

In Japan, drastically expand access to Asian languages

Internationalization can be fostered through transnational innovations

Promote high school and collegiate exchanges that include three or more distinctive cultural experiences

Establish an Asia-wide university

Expand opportunities for virtual worlds

Involve beneficiaries

Cultivate greater funding from the corporate community

Challenge local communities and NGOs to devote more funding and organization to new linkages

Encourage businesses to give attention to international skills in personnel decisions and articulate the desirability of these skills

Develop tax and other incentives, such as matching funds

Table 3.1 highlights the major areas for improvement, starting with the nature of images, looking at obstacles to access, settling in, and then focusing on more programmatic challenges. Here, we offer a few illustrations.

Images. A major goal of international education is to improve understanding, but sometimes the knowledge young people have is so distorted that they are unwilling to consider learning more about a foreign setting. For example, many American youth still think of Japan as akin to an alien planet where women wear kimonos and prepare tea and where raw fish and other exotic dishes are the only food available. The news media foster these images through advertisements of Japanese products and their coverage of Japanese news, which tends to stress the extraordinary over the ordinary. Typical news stories talk of youth suicide or of high school prostitution in Japan without reference to the United States, where the rates for these social pathologies are much higher. Young Americans are told Japan is an expensive place where it is difficult to have much fun, even though young Japanese, especially during their collegiate days, are easily as carefree as young Americans. The scarcity of UUnited States news about Japan is shocking, as is its quality.

In contrast, Japanese news media provide much more extensive coverage of the United States Major Japanese newspapers have numerous correspondents resident in the United States, and they publish much news, especially about United States political and economic developments. However, the Japanese coverage of more mundane topics such as everyday living in the U.S. is not as extensive, and this may lead to false images. Young Japanese are told that America is a dangerous place, and as the following story suggests there is some truth in these tales. So there is a tendency for young Japanese to seek exchange experiences in safe, racially homogeneous rural locales; many thus miss the excitement of America's dynamic urban settings, where the majority of Americans live.

Fewer Students Studying Abroad Since Hattori's Death

The number of Japanese high school students studying abroad in fiscal 1994 dropped for the first time since such statistics have been kept, an Education Ministry report said Wednesday. A total of 3,998 high school students studied abroad in fiscal 1994 for more than three months, 489 fewer than in fiscal 1992, when the ministry took the previous survey. The decline was particularly sharp in the United States, which attracted 593 fewer students in fiscal 1994 for a total of 2,346. The sharp fall came after the fatal shooting of a Japanese exchange student, Yoshihiro Hattori, in Baton Rouge, La., in October, 1992.

From Story in Japan Times, Feb. 8, P. 2

Information. In recent years, there has been a rapid expansion in the number of opportunities for study in Japan as well as in the financial support available for young people who desire such opportunities. Much of this information is available on the Internet or from specialized agencies. Yet it is not at all clear how a young person, with average computer literacy or knowledge of Japan, should go about accessing this information. The typical high school youth has access only if the local high school has a direct tie with a high school in Japan, and the typical collegiate youth gains *entrée* drawing on the advice of his study-abroad counselor. In other words, the more systematic efforts to compile information are still beyond the access of the average person.

Infrastructure. Many American universities and colleges have had several decades of experience in admitting students from other countries, and have had the opportunity to develop relatively elaborate procedures and facilities for receiving these students. The University of Chicago, Columbia, and UC-Berkeley have special International Houses where foreign students can rent rooms and dine together. Most universities have international offices staffed by specialists who help foreign students with their visa problems and provide special advise on registering for courses, taking care of their health, and learning about American customs (through special clinics, host-family visits, and other measures). These services are not as well-developed in Japan, though in recent years there have been major improvements. Other infrastructure issues include the obstacles youth of both nations encounter when they seek visas for overseas study, the special costs they encounter when seeking health care, and the challenges they face when opening up bank accounts.

Vertical articulation. The most obvious outcome of the ad hoc evolution of international education is the poor articulation between programs. In the United States, international education is most developed at the tertiary level, with colleges and universities having large international offices and extensive area studies programs. Between Harvard and MIT there are more than 35 academic chairs endowed by funds originating in Japan, and both of these institutions have popular programs in Japanese language and area studies. Yet in the broader Boston area, there are only two high schools that offer the Japanese language (one of which is a private institution). In other words, despite the extensive resources for international education at the collegiate level, there is virtually no outreach to the secondary-level public schools. This same pattern is repeated in many other parts of the United States.

Japan's articulation problems are different, focusing largely around the university entrance exams. These exams treat competence in English as an essential criterion for university admissions, but in most instances they fail to acknowledge the importance of non-European languages such as Korean, Thai, or Indonesian. Partly for that reason, few high school students become motivated to devote time to these languages.

In both systems, there is poor articulation between the employment sector, where there is a growing need for young people with Transnational Competence, and the educational sector, which has the primary responsibility for developing the skills of young people. Greater coordination between these sectors would do much to enhance the vitality of international education.

Horizontal integration. In Japan, the more centralized educational system facilitates the communication of new instructional material on international education and language instruction between high schools. In contrast, in America's highly decentralized system, each school district is on its own in the development of new programs and materials; some coordination is now emerging under the auspices of both the Japan Foundation and the Association of Asian Studies, but much more needs to be done. At the collegiate level, individual institutions of both nations largely operate independently, setting exchange agreements with specific counterparts. This leads to much inefficiency in terms of management costs for student exchanges and the fact that students are often unavailable for these exchanges. While colleges with exchange programs may not have students ready to go, there are many other colleges without such programs that have interested students. Japan is extreme in this regard; four out of every five students who go to the United States do not utilize the established exchange relations. To reduce costs and make better use of opportunities, consortia involving groups of institutions may prove more effective.

Program quality and transnational innovations. The focus of many current exchange programs is on language and culture, with some attention to international relations. Yet the dominant theme in current U.S.-Japan interactions is competitiveness in technology, trade, and capital. New opportunities need to be developed that reflect the current realities. These opportunities may stress classroom instruction, but they also need to recognize the active-learning styles of today's youth by offering opportunities for internships in corporate settings and research laboratories. A special challenge is to develop programs that facilitate transnational experiences through encouraging meetings and negotiations between young people of diverse cultural backgrounds in a variety of geographic settings. In other words, there is a growing need for programs that enable young people to study and work in several local settings that span as many national boundaries. Such programs require considerable preparation and flexible infrastructure.

Involve beneficiaries. As depicted in Table 2.2, contemporary international education tends to benefit individuals, universities, nations, and humanity, and the costs of these programs have tended to be born by those entities. At the graduate level, the share born by governments has been relatively large, while at the collegiate and community levels, the other beneficiaries have contributed relatively more. Looking to the 21st century, the corporate or industrial sector emerges as a prominent beneficiary of international education, and this sector needs to become more involved both in program development and in funding. Professionals in the field of international education need to devise new strategies for reaching out to corporate beneficiaries. These might include unique programs designed for the needs of particular companies or industrial sectors, special opportunities to share information about overseas settings for corporate activity, and/or joint cooperation in developing new legislation for tax exemptions or other related considerations.

Summing Up: Is the U.S. System in Decline?

The fact-finding phase of the project identified several notable strengths and weaknesses in the U.S. approach to international education, which we will consider in greater detail in Chapter Four:

• Low high school enrollments in foreign languages and world history courses result in a weak base of preparation and motivation for transnational learning experiences.

• Despite this weakness at the high school level, public and nonprofit funding in the United States for transnational learning experiences has been concentrated at the tertiary level.

• At many American tertiary-level institutions, the major thrust is to bring more foreign students to the United States, rather than to prepare Americans for overseas exposure.

• While the U.S. government, through its overseas cultural centers and its efficient issuance of student visas, has encouraged foreign students to choose American higher education, recent legislation and budgetary cuts for the USIA and the Immigration and Naturalization Service (INS), are making the United States appear a less hospitable place for foreign students.

• The U.S. colleges and universities that feature Asian studies tend to focus on elite preparation and insist on exceptionally high standards of language preparation that discourage all but the most ambitious students.

• While U.S. community and educational institutions establish numerous exchange agreements with Japanese and Asian institutions, they rarely implement these agreements. For example, at the collegiate level more than 500 agreements have been established between U.S. and Japanese institutions, but students do not participate in many of them.

• U.S. corporate leaders speak of a global marketplace, and they frequently assert the need for a new labor force that can operate in this marketplace; yet most corporations place no priority on language skills and international experience when hiring new recruits for their managerial or technical tracks.

• National funding and political support for international studies is waning.

Summing Up: Japan's Narrow International Focus

On the **Japanese side**, the following are some problem areas that will be addressed in Chapter Five:

• Japanese education has a narrow focus on the English language and on European studies, to the virtual exclusion of Asia.

• While large numbers of Japanese go overseas for study (mainly to the United States), very few of those in the elite course of Japan's top national universities have this opportunity; rather, they are locked during their pre-collegiate days in exam preparation and in their collegiate days in a highly domesticated educational experience.

• Most of Japan's universities have a minimal infrastructure for helping their students learn about overseas study opportunities and to receive foreign students; also, the Japanese government places many obstacles in the way of foreign youth who seek to study in Japan.

• The traditional focus of Japanese programs has been on what is good for Japan, with less attention to what is good for particular local areas or communities.

• A major counterbalance to these weaknesses is the exceptional energy of Japan's Ministry of Education in devising new ways to encourage transnational learning in both young Japanese and youth from other countries.

Conclusion

In this chapter we have introduced a framework for the systemic analysis of international education, and we have summarized several of the key conclusions from our fact-finding studies of contemporary U.S. and Japanese activities. In the next two chapters, we will propose a number of improvements to promote greater Transnational Competence in these two national settings.

Chapter Four

Redesign and Development: New Linkages

A variety of studies have looked at the U.S.-Japan exchange relationship, and all concur that more exposure of U.S. students and citizens to Japan is desirable. Japan plays an increasingly important role in the transnational activities that influence everyday life and commerce in the United States, and thus more Americans need to have a deeper understanding of the workings of Japanese society. Whatever the category of exchange, far more Japanese come to the United States than do Americans go to Japan. The imbalances are troubling, but they are best thought of as symptoms of more systemic weaknesses, as outlined in Chapter Three. Redesigning the exchange relationship between the United States and Japan will require both short-term and long-term improvements. Neither the United States nor Japan has the exchange tradition that Europe has, for example, and there has been little coordination, with each nation pretty much going its own way. In this chapter we focus on those improvements that are likely to help Americans improve their understanding of Japan and of Japan's role in the new transnational world.

Images and Realities: Improving Information

As is always the case when two cultures interact, there is an inherent tendency to gravitate toward the stereotypical, to simplify and, as a result, to utilize images that distort rather than enhance one's understanding of a complex society These problems exist along a spectrum that ranges from formal scholarship to journalism (although it appears in more extreme form in the latter). America's formal scholarship on Japan often focuses on the highly specific and does not strengthen our understanding of the popular culture. America's journalism often focuses on the sensational and bizarre and thus must be challenged when overstepping the bounds of responsibility. The point here is that there is a need to further assure that the images we create of Japan reflect the complex realities of that society. An obvious first step in adjusting prevailing images is to reassess the information and knowledge dimension of the relationship. It is not likely that an increase in the quality and quantity of the exchange relationship will occur, unless both sides have accurate and easy-to-access information regarding existing exchange opportunities. Information and knowledge should not be restricted to exchanges, but should be inclusive to encompass broad areas of general knowledge about each society and culture, including language study. It has become a truism today to speak of knowledge as power, and knowledge as the key to success—the information age in all its complexity. This is the stance that has been taken by business, but ironically enough, it is the educational community that appears to be lagging behind.

In the broad area of U.S.-Japan exchange relations, we find here too that in the information and knowledge dimension, the U.S. has some catching up to do. Most broadly speaking, and somewhat ironically, it appears that it is the United States that is more insular in its world outlook; Japan, the island nation known for its insularity in other ways, is most outward-looking internationally. As Altbach points out (1995), knowledge and information are directly related to the desire to learn more about a subject. A recent Carnegie study shows that professors in Japan feel strongly the need to know about world trends and development in other countries, particularly the United States. The data are less supportive of U.S. professors sharing the same feeling.

There are a number of measures of this imbalance, language being the most obvious, as many more Japanese study English than Americans study Japanese (or any other foreign language, for that matter). English is required in Japan from junior high through high school. Many of those who continue to college also continue to study English. By contrast, less than one percent of high school students study Japanese in the United States and only about 70,000 post-secondary students study Japanese. It did not seem strange for Americans to encourage and even require a European language (or Latin) as a legacy to that time when U.S. economic and political interests were so clearly tied to Europe. Now that a dramatic shift has occurred toward the Pacific with Japan as the lead nation (soon to be eclipsed by China), it should not seem strange to put much more emphasis on the early acquisition of Japanese (and Chinese) as a necessary prerequisite for students preparing for the global marketplace (much of it in Asia) that they will enter when their schooling is complete.

Apart from language, general knowledge about the United States in Japan is simply much greater than knowledge about Japan in the United States. This is a result not only of the largely disproportionate numbers of Japanese who visit, work, and study in the United States, but also because of the greater availability of numerous other knowledge sources. For example, in 1994 the number of books translated from English to Japanese was 2,295. In the United States the number of Japanese books translated from Japanese to English was 33. One could argue that the productivity of original books in the United States is simply greater and hence there is less need for translated books; but even concerning original books in the respective settings, the U.S. edge is modest. What appears to be happening here is a lingering sense that if something is important it will be written in English in the first place. The truth is, by not engaging in a systematic translation process, the United States is missing out on a rich and informative variety of publications, both popular and scientific, that would greatly increase our knowledge of Japan and allow the United States to interact with the Japanese on a much more level playing field. In general, "knowledge products" are coming from the United States to Japan at a much greater rate than vice versa.

Central to increasing and improving our knowledge bases would be to determine what agencies currently exist, on both sides, to provide timely and accurate information regarding the variety of exchanges we are concerned with here. Currently, there is no adequate inventory of agencies that could be contacted, although many such agencies exist (i.e., the Japan Society for Promotion of Science, the Japan-U.S. Educational Commission-Fulbright, the Japan Foundation, the U.S. National Science Foundation, etc.). Lacking such a comprehensive and critical inventory, it is virtually impossible to make sense of the bewildering variety of exchange programs that currently exist (as of 1992 Japanese colleges and universities had signed 2,722 exchange agreements—907 with a U.S. partner and 527 with China) (Altbach and Umakoshi, 1995). All of this is uncoordinated, so as a first step in improving the information conduit, a joint bilateral effort to construct such a critical inventory is essential.

Improving information involves more than just finding out what kind of programs exist and where. A second stage would involve a broad process of "knowledge creation and distribution," a wide range which includes exchanges of books, catalogues, journals, the recognition of "invisible colleges" of colleagues who have worked together for years on joint projects, ad hoc invitations to lecture in each country, and the increasing use of the Internet, Web pages, and e-mail as a form of popular and scholarly communication between the two nations. As Altbach and Umakoshi (1995, p. 8) have stated: "We need to inventory the sources of knowledge creations and dissemination, analyze the interrelationships among these sources, and then ensure that there is adequate and sustained support."

The question will still be asked, however, "Why do we need to know more about Japan?" While there are many answers to this question, including simply that it is obvious when one looks at economic, strategic and political data (more than just the trade statistics), the emergence of Japan as an important player in the global science and technology (S&T) arena is one of the more compelling reasons to be informed. While the share of world science being produced in Japan is not large, it has increased dramatically from 4 to 8 percent while the substantial U.S. share has fallen from 42 to 35 percent. It is difficult to predict how far this trend will continue, but the work being done in Japan in S&T is important and increasing, and U.S. corporations and scientists are generally unaware of this development.

By contrast, Japanese corporations and scientists are far more active in exploring channels of communication and knowledge of U.S. activities. This level of knowledge access is critical, for as Reich (1991) has argued, what will matter most in the future is not the borders that surround us as nations, but rather the "skills and insights" that our human resources possess, the knowledge and information about the world around us and in critical nation-states such as Japan. In general, what this means for the corporation is obtaining accurate and useful information through analysis of annual reports, trade journals, technical literature and other sources, visits to international settings, recruiting international staff, investing in international technologies and firms, and establishing foreign subsidiaries. Each of these activities requires new sets of skills for employees to acquire, including language and area skills. It is not clear that U.S. corporations have recognized this reality.

In some respects, the respective roles of the United States and Japan have shifted. In the past, Japan saw itself as lagging behind the United States in S&T and therefore devoted extensive resources to information-gathering and education and technical exchange in order to catch up. The situation is not exactly reversed, but Japan is advanced in some critical areas and the United States has not generally accepted the fact that it needs to engage in similar information-gathering if it is to stay abreast and excel where it has a comparative advantage. For example, there is no U.S. equivalent to the Japan Information Center for S&T (JICST), which translates key international S&T material. In pure statistical terms, the imbalance between acquisition of S&T knowledge through scientific and technical interchange can be summed up this way: As of 1991, 72,000 Japanese researchers came to the United States and 5,000 U.S. counterparts went to Japan. Forty-seven percent of all Japanese researchers come to the United States and only 6 percent of those received by Japan come from the United States. One net result of this imbalance is that Japan generally leads the United States in technical innovation and product development. As Cummings and Nakayama (1995) suggest, one possible explanation for this phenomenon is that one team has more familiarity with its competitors' practices than the other.

Proposals to narrow the information gap are not difficult to suggest. A general suggestion and one that we will return to later in this chapter is focused on the response that higher education can make in the continued training of area specialists and the offering of area and language programs focused on Japan for those majoring in technical, business and other non-area studies fields. There are some positive indicators on this front, with increasing numbers of U.S. institutions with Japan-oriented programs (328 in 1989 to 482 in 1995) and increasing numbers of doctoral dissertations on Japan. Much of this increase, however, can be credited to support given by the Japan Foundation. Thus, in the United States it is necessary to assure continued support of interdisciplinary Japan studies centers, the steady production of scholars who can teach in these areas, good library facilities for the study of Japan, increased opportunities for U.S. students to go to Japan to study, and financial support for advanced graduate study. These represent basic preconditions to provide accurate and informed information flows about Japan to the United States.

Other proposals would include the following:

Increased Japanese language training in the United States; basic as well as advanced
Increased translation of Japanese materials of all types, but especially in the S&T area, into English
Increased flow of "knowledge products" —books, periodicals, e-mail, etc.—to the United States from Japan
A reduction of structural impediments on both sides, but particularly Japan, to gaining access to information
More coordinated effort to provide timely and accurate information about the availability of research and study opportunities, as well as agencies that can assist in this effort
An increased focus on the S&T area as one that holds great promise for providing mutually beneficial linkages

Providing a more comprehensive information base is an important prerequisite, but it is not sufficient given the obsolete and convoluted current state of the infrastructure within which the application of such information must occur. Major reform is needed, and to this topic we now turn.

Improving the Infrastructure

We have just discussed a major component of the infrastructure, the knowledge dimension, and found it lacking particularly in the United States.

But the basic architecture of our exchange programs is also fraught with infrastructure problems. Among the many efforts that have been made to increase the numbers of U.S. students going to Japan is the phenomenon of U.S. "branch" campuses established in Japan. The branch campus experience also illustrates the nature of structural impediments within the infrastructure.

During the American university boom in the late 1980s, numerous branch campuses were established as a new, innovative mechanism to encourage American students to study in Japan in more familiar surroundings. They were also seen as mechanisms to attract Japanese students so that they could more easily transfer to the United States. With a few high-quality and enduring exceptions, many of these efforts have since largely failed due to a combination of factors and problems unforeseen by the U.S. campuses and their Japanese partners:

- naiveté in negotiations
- unmet educational expectations
- downgrading of educational standards
- shallow instructional commitment
- complex governance arrangements
- budgets based on marginal cost
- financial and legal obstacles
- groups on both sides seeking to control information and access

There are additional infrastructure problems, as well. Again, the S&T issue arises and the nature of the problem is slightly different from that raised above. The infrastructure in the United States that provides for an even flow of information and human resources between the United States and Japan in the S&T area has been flawed and intermittent. The U.S. government has taken several steps to fix this aspect of the infrastructure by urging Congress, for example, to pass the Japanese Technical Literature Act in 1986 to provide a resource for the translation of Japanese technical data, but efforts have been limited and sporadic and it appears they attract little attention outside government. The big question has been about who should take the lead in these efforts. Two natural possible leaders are the U.S. Department of Commerce and U.S. corporations. The view of Commerce is that the market should lead, thus throwing the ball back into the corporate court (Cummings and Nakayama, 1995).

Another such effort has been the EAGLE project (Engineering Alliance for Engineering Education, 1988), which brought together 15 schools of engineering in the United States to identify promising engineering students, provide them with a special course in Japanese and place them in internship positions in Japan for part of their study period. The National Security Education Program is another "national defense" inspired program designed to create a cadre of language specialists in Japanese. The futures of these programs have been under seige and neither has generated substantial interest or support from the corporate sector.

Most of these governmental efforts to fix the infrastructure with respect to S&T are too new to determine if they have been working well enough.

What seems to be needed is a wholesale formative evaluation effort focused on these and other programs to determine their level of success. What is also needed is a strategy to engage the corporate sector more fully so that a) they are aware of the programs that exist, and 2) they begin to interact with them or initiate new and better programs. By way of contrast, the Japanese seem to have done much better at creating an integrated infrastructure for focusing on S&T in the United States, complete with an elaborate set of listening posts. They have effectively created a tripartite alliance of academic, government and business enterprises to support this effort and analyze the information gleaned. The close relations that leading science and technology professionals in Japan maintain with corporate research labs know no parallel in the United States. The lead seems to have been taken by the private sector in Japan (the largest number of Japanese researchers coming to the United States are financed and supported by the Japanese corporate structure), and it is our conclusion that the same should be true in the United States. It is not likely that the government will take much of a lead for spending funds for such an infrastructure.

Reforming High School Education

Some would argue, with a certain justification, that the issues we are discussing here would best be addressed by first examining the status of high school education in the United States. Redressing the imbalances of the U.S.-Japan educational exchange relationship is not likely to see much improvement without some significant changes in the early preparation of students for the global society they are about to face upon graduation. We have to acknowledge at the outset that this is a difficult area and one that will be troublesome to change. There is already great pressure on the U.S. curriculum, with an avowed priority being placed in most communities on basic education, especially mathematics and science. The addition of new curricular areas that will address the internationalism issue will certainly face great obstacles. But we believe that recent educational reform in the United States has largely ignored language and international education, and these curricular areas deserve high priority.

Concerning high school study of the Japanese language, in 1994 only 500

U.S. high schools (or three percent of all high schools) offered a class in Japan, and often the teachers of these classes had a part-time status and were inadequately trained. Only 42,000 students (less than one percent of all high school students) took a class in Japanese. Currently, in the United States, 98 percent of what foreign language instruction exists is in Spanish, French, German or Latin. Spanish alone accounts for 61 percent of all foreign languages taught. For every one student studying Japanese in the American high school, there are fifty students studying Spanish. The proposal here is not to decrease the study of Spanish or the culture of Spanish-speaking societies, for they also have an increasingly important link to the United States. Rather it is urged that much greater attention be focused on Japan (and Asia) in the American high school curriculum.

The going will not be easy. The United States is the only advanced industrial nation in the world where one can graduate from college without having had one year of a foreign language. The United States is basically a nation with no planned or developed language policy. Most other developed nations have an established policy and are therefore proactive when it comes to language issues; the United States continues to be reactive. The policies that do exist in the United States are fragmented and dominated by states and local boards. Here again, a joint concerted effort by both the private sector and the national government to target critical languages (those critical to economic competitiveness, for example) and encourage local districts to do more with foreign languages might result in some increased interest in languages such as Japanese.

Efforts to reform high school curricula with respect to early exposure to the study of Japan and Japanese will not be easy. If foreign language instruction is to increase either through inclusion in some form of national standards or through individual state-level reform (or both), the case can and should be strongly made for increased efforts in the study of Japanese and perhaps other Asian languages. Just as it was common practice to offer European languages in the United States throughout the 1900s because that was where the political economy was most strongly linked, the case can be more than made that in the second millennium the U.S. political economy is clearly going to be linked to Asia and the study of Japanese and Chinese should be just as common as the study of French and German was in the 1900s.

A consistent U.S. policy toward the study of foreign languages would be a good first step, as would a common foreign language requirement for graduation from high school. A more creative use of distance learning would also be useful, utilizing new technology such as the Internet, and modeling on such successful programs as the Satellite Education Resources Consortium in

Nebraska, the Satellite Telecom Educational Program (STEP) in Washington, the Texas Interactive Institutional Network (TI-IN) in Texas, the Oregon immersion program and others would help other interested states make progress in this direction. The benefits in terms of redressing the current exchange imbalance between the United States and Japan would be substantial.

Modifying Collegiate and Graduate School Opportunities

The bulk of those participating in U.S.-Japan exchange relations are college students at either the undergraduate or graduate levels. And the majority of these exchanges are junior-year-abroad programs. As has already been noted, these numbers are small and appear to have plateaued; a variety of measures can be taken to expand them. The issue here is that historically, those students from the United States who opt to participate in one or another of the many collegiate-level exchange programs do so to study Japanese language and culture. They are majoring in some form of area studies at an American university, either through an area studies center or program, or one of the social science or humanities disciplines with a focus on Japan. This phenomenon correlates highly with the dramatic increase in the study of Japanese in the United States already referred to; from 1987 to 1991, Japanese language study grew at a dramatic rate of 95 percent. As the Japan-U.S. Cultural Committee (1992, p. 7) report states: "If captured in the right manner, this surge in language enrollments could translate into large numbers of Americans studying in Japan." Furthermore, the MLA (Modern Language Association) reports that the growth of the study of Japanese has outdistanced growth in all other foreign languages, and this usually correlates with study abroad. It appears, however, that this continued interest in the study of Japan and Japanese has not been captured in the right manner, since the number of such students who pursue Japanese language study abroad has not kept pace with the growth in language study at home.

It is suggested that one reason there has not been such a sustained high correlation is that there may be a bad fit between the curriculum of the study-abroad programs and the curricular interests of those studying the Japanese language. One bit of evidence supporting this assertion is that the National Foreign Language Center found that 32 percent of college Japanese language students indicated that business was their prime motivation for studying Japanese; yet few study-abroad programs offer business as a course of study.

Indeed, the basic curriculum for most study-abroad programs consists of two parts: 1) Japanese language study (for which there is a problem in finding qualified Japanese language teachers), and 2) academic courses, the bulk of which are taught in English, with the corresponding problem of finding

Japanese professors qualified to teach in English (DeCoker et al, 1992). The teaching of Japanese consists of between 30-60 percent of the curriculum of study-abroad programs, and the academic courses are typically focused on Japanese studies; instruction is in the typical American lecture-discussion format (DeCoker et al, 1992). Options do exist in a limited number of cases to allow junior-year-abroad students to enroll in regular courses. In this light, DeCoker and his colleagues suggest:

1) more diversified Japanese language courses for students at all levels,
2) more diversity of academic courses for students depending on their knowledge level,
3) course offerings that are a closer fit to the curriculum in the home university in the United States,
4) a teacher-student ratio more like the United States, and
5) for those U.S. students with adequate Japanese language skills, the option and ease of enrolling in regular courses in the Japanese university (DeCoker et al, 1992).

The other institutional issue restricting the curriculum for U.S. study-abroad students in Japan is the assertion that only the private universities have established special programs for U.S. undergraduates who want to study Japanese history, language and culture. By and large, the national universities have not established such programs, although some national universities have established *ryugakusei sentas,* which offer one-year programs for *nikkensei,* but these centers are quite limited in number (Homma, 1993).

Two other emerging areas of study deserve mention and more research. There appear to be increasing numbers of full-scale special programs, taught in English, in the areas of science and engineering. These are being offered at the national universities at a total, as of 1993, of 14 faculties, institutes, or graduate schools (Homma, 1993). For example, the civil engineering faculty of Tokyo University offers courses in English, which are attracting talented U.S. graduate students.

The second area, business, has already been alluded to. While little was offered at the time of the Homma survey, it is recommended that this would be a fertile area to develop. The CULCON report of September 1, 1990, is cited as evidence that 32 percent of American students studying in Japan are interested in the formal study of business; 48 percent want to work in business after graduation. Homma believes a joint business-university collaboration would be worth pursuing (Homma, 1993).[11]

---

[11] The CIBER programs in the United States funded by Title VI, are responding to this need somewhat as they forge linkages with Japanese firms to send MBA students for Internships in Japan.

Indeed, some innovative programs to link the study of Japan with student interest in business have been initiated on several U.S. campuses and seem to hold promise for modestly increasing the numbers of American students going to Japan. Often attached to schools of business and management, these programs (some of which are part of the CIBER initiative of NDEA Title VI) seek to blend language and area studies with standard business degrees, both undergraduate and M.B.A.s. One of the leading programs in this respect is the IMF (International Management Fellows) Program of the Anderson School of Management at UCLA. This program, like many others, is designed to prepare students for the global business environment. It consists of a 24-month certificate program offered through CIBER, and is intended to provide fellows with the capacity to function effectively in an international context. This is accomplished by combining in-classroom M.B.A. training with a variety of overseas experiences in international business.

Although the structure of these programs differs from university to university, they generally begin in June prior to the start of the regular M.B.A. program, and continue through graduation two years later. Over the course of the program students spend more than eight months abroad doing 1) intensive language study, 2) seminars on sociocultural issues, 3) business courses at a local graduate management school, and 4) an in-country internship.

It appears that these programs offer great promise for selectively increasing the numbers of U.S. students studying in Japan. They respond to the data which show that increasing numbers of Americans want to go to Japan not for Japanese studies per se, but for more functional purposes (business, engineering, science and technology). Response to the programs has been encouraging. However, several important issues remain to be resolved. Those programs that seem to have done the best have offered the international component as a certificate, rather than a separate or joint degree. This reality is probably a function of studies that show that American CEOs have priorities quite different from those of their Japanese and European counterparts. These priorities are carried throughout the corporate structure. As a result, U.S. corporate recruiters will tend to place much higher emphasis on technical business skills than on linguistic or cultural skills. This is in contrast to Western Europe, Japan and Latin America, where more than 80 percent of CEOs indicated that foreign language skills were "very important" to their recruitment policies, compared with about 20 percent of U.S. CEOs (Korn, 1994).

Another factor that is critical to continued success of these programs is the cost of the internship component. Many of the programs are requiring that this cost be borne by the company providing the internship and at a level that allows the student to live comfortably in the target country. As might be expected, this reduces the number of participating countries and therefore limits the quantity of students who can participate in the program. Yet, companies are responding and, in the case of the UCLA program, represent a wide cross-section of corporate experiences (e.g., Citibank, Marubeni Trading Corp., Mattel Inc., Mellon Bank, United Airlines, etc.).

From Area Studies to Issue Studies

Historically, as we have seen, area studies programs, Japanese studies in particular, and the universities and foundations that have supported them have been the principal preparatory track for students desiring to participate in a U.S.-Japan exchange program. In recent years, however, the concept of area studies, Japanese studies included, has been undergoing a transformation at the collegiate, governmental, and foundation levels. The transformation has prompted suggestions that area studies be completely replaced by issue or problem studies, while die-hard supporters of area studies in a traditional sense defend the original programs. Rather than view this transformation as a further obstacle to increasing U.S.-Japan exchanges, we believe it provides a unique challenge and opportunity to strengthen and increase the quantity and quality of such exchanges.

A little background is in order, however. For several decades the principal vehicles for the study of Japan were the many high-quality area studies programs in a variety of distinguished U.S. universities. These programs came under several rubrics, including degree programs in East Asian Studies, separate Centers for Japanese Studies, and broader Asian Studies Programs. What they all had in common was a curricular emphasis on the intensive interdisciplinary study of Japanese language, history and culture. Prompted by post-World War II concerns about U.S. preparedness in the Asian/Pacific region, these programs were supported by both U.S. governmental and private foundations, and well-endowed centers and library collections emerged on many of the nation's best campuses. A generation of experts and scholars were trained in this area studies model, receiving B.A. and M.A. degrees in East Asian Studies, Asian Studies and Japanese Studies, or some variation thereof. These students and graduates also constituted a primary flow of U.S. students and scholars to Japan, where they furthered their studies onsite. Our problem today is that we continue to think of U.S.-Japan exchanges in terms that are no longer altogether accurate. As Koppel (1995) notes:

Today it is clear that the future of intellectual leadership for studies on Asia is not necessarily with programs of Asian studies. One indicator is that in the 1990s, about one of 10 students going to Asia each year to do dissertation research in the social sciences or humanities will receive a doctorate in Asian studies or one of its subregional fields, compared with one in seven students in the early 1980s. It is consistent with a recognized trend over the last decade: the increasing use of the disciplines for pursuing graduate interests in scholarship on Asia.

While the picture has changed, it is somewhat more complex than a simple shift from area studies to discipline studies. In fact, area studies and Japanese studies continue to exist on most major campuses, and in fact are flourishing on some. The recognition that one must have in-depth knowledge of language, history and culture if one is to effectively apply disciplinary skills or professional skills is increasing. Other foundations are now supporting efforts to internationalize the disciplines which they view as having become too narrow and parochial (Ford and Mellon, for example). And a variety of cross-disciplinary efforts has emerged among certain disciplines to address this narrowness, efforts that indicate that there is enough intellectual ground between area studies and the disciplines to stake some claims and do some new things.

One promising trend is for area studies centers (which now do not often offer degrees) to focus their work on research efforts that cross boundaries, that center on transdisciplinary forms of inquiry and direct their efforts toward thematic and problem-oriented areas of inquiry (e.g., environment, health, trade, migration, democratization, etc.). The effective merging of area studies with good disciplinary and cross-disciplinary work allows both camps to attract and recruit students who have a desire to learn more about Japan in the context of their chosen profession, thus expanding the base of students and scholars to Japan, rather than limiting it. This is not to say that building such strategic alliances between the disciplines and area studies will be an easy task. As Koppel (1995) has noted, there is both competition and convergence between area and disciplines in the U.S. university, but that does not mean there is a lack of common ground for creatively approaching the issues of U.S.-Japan exchanges. Administrative units governing area studies centers at major campuses such as UCLA, UCB, University of Washington, University of Illinois and so on are moving in this direction and building effective new alliances that are gradually translating into increased and higher-quality flows of students and scholars to Japan and other world regions. This trend should be encouraged and communicated to the foundations and government agencies, which in turn could target their support toward these efforts. It therefore remains for the university, government, and foundation communities to rise to this challenge and find ways to approach the study of Japan in new contexts.

Linkages: Changing the Structure

From the foregoing it is clear that a new model for exchange is necessary. The new model should encompass the realities and complexities of both interest in and support for international exchanges, and seek to provide for a greater integration of the key actors in the process—strong, self-sustaining, horizontal linkages. The bilateral, government-dominated, institution-to-institution approach of past years, an approach that saw the private sector (apart from foundations) essentially standing on the sidelines, has gradually and not so gradually been dismantled as both governments and various levels of education (school districts and higher education institutions) have experienced one or more varieties of downsizing. This has been less of a conscious restructuring than a disordered retreat from a decades-old archetype of international exchange.

Nothing so far has emerged to take the place of a system heavily dominated by government funding and bilateral exchange agreements. Nevertheless, higher education in the United States and Japan has been changing in response to the forces described above, and several interesting and encouraging cases have emerged that contain within them elements of a new realignment of actors that together are providing support for United States and Japan exchanges. The model that is emerging is a variation on previous approaches to international exchanges but focuses on two principal themes: linkages in the broadest sense, and tripartite alliances between government, higher education, and the private sector.

In some respects the changes that are taking place in higher education and other educational sectors, not only in the United States but in Japan as well, mimic to some degree changes that have been occurring in the private sector for about a decade. Variously termed "global strategies," "strategic alliances," and "networking," these strategies have been employed at the corporate level in response to a dramatically altered business climate where "going it alone" can be disastrous (*Global Strategies*, 1994). Kenichi Ohmae (1989) recognizes "that in a complex, uncertain world filled with dangerous opponents, it is best not to go it alone" (p. 109). He argues for building alliances, entente, between complex players in the corporate world to better serve customers (not as a quick fix for lagging profits) in the long-term. Alliances are a modern necessity not only because it is not possible for one entity to do it all, but because consumers demand them.

While companies have been utilizing strategic alliances and networks for several years, educational institutions have been slower to recognize the potential of these mechanisms. Certainly there have been alliances, exchange agreements, formal and informal networks between educational institutions, but less so between education, government and the private sector. It is suggested here that movement in the creative application of strategic alliances and networks among this triad of actors would increase the possibility of enhancing both the quality and quantity of exchanges between the United

States and Japan. Some of the crucial ideas contained in the experience of business and corporate global alliance strategies may provide an interesting new approach to educational exchanges. As has been the case with business, it is not likely that universities and other educational entities will be able to go it alone to increase the flow of students in one or another direction.

It is also not likely that bilateral arrangements between government funding agencies and educational institutions will continue to provide the engine that is necessary to drive exchanges in new and better directions. And the rather passive role that the private sector has played will have to be challenged if movement is to occur. Some risk will be involved as universities, government agencies and the private sector seek to support international exchanges and find ways to ally themselves (loss of some autonomy on the part of universities and government agencies, financial risk on the part of the private sector) for the purposes of advancing international exchanges, but the alternative will be a continuing decline in both quality and quantity of exchanges.

Some common characteristics (to paraphrase Perlmutter and Heenan, 1986) of strategic alliances or partnerships between the private sector and educational institutions are:

1. Two or more entities focus on a common, long-term strategy with international dimensions to achieve a common goal.
2. The relationship between the various entities is reciprocal; each partner shares his specific strengths with the other.
3. The partner's efforts cross conceptual and functional boundaries.
4. The relationship is horizontal, rather than vertical, characterized by knowledge and resource exchanges and other combinations.
5. Each partner retains his identity and autonomy while cooperating to achieve common goals.

From the Nation to the Community, the Corporation, the College

The respective roles of the principal actors in educational exchanges—nations, local communities, corporations, and higher educational institutions—have shifted rather dramatically over the past several years. The traditional model of national governments paving the way with significantly funded exchange programs, drawing local communities and educational institutions along with them, has given way to a decline in national involvement, an increase in local community-initiated activities, higher educational institutions seeking alternative sources of support, and the corporate sector just beginning to see a role for itself.

Nation-states have weakened generally in the past decade. This can be observed in the world of business where some suggest that "giant global companies have already lost their national identities and have replaced national sovereignty" (Kanter, 1994, p. 229), and in the world of international relations where a variety of association configurations are now as important as the nation-state once was (APEC, ASEAN, NAFTA, United Europe, etc.). What are the implications for educational exchanges of this development? It is likely, as Wollons and Abe (1996) suggest, local efforts to increase both the quantity and quality of international exchanges, specifically exchanges between the United States and Japan, will play an increasingly important role. Furthermore, this role will deviate from the former reliance on bilateral relations and become increasingly multilateral. One specific trend in this direction is that the number of sister city relationships between Japan and China are increasing, suggesting that the United States would be wise to begin to engage in triadic relations, rather than concentrating only on U.S.-Japan exchanges. The community or grassroots approaches are likely to increase in importance and play a major role in U.S.-Japan exchange relations.

What about the role of the corporate sector? The corporate sector, of course, has been involved in U.S.-Japan exchanges all along, but in a haphazard and unpredictable way. As Cummings and Nakayama (1995) note, there has been a surprising lack of interest at the corporate level in recognizing the value that can be gained from increased knowledge about Japan. This is from the United States side. The Japanese, on the other hand, seem less reluctant to support exchange activities. Evidence suggests that the view of U.S. corporations is changing and that there is more willingness to support exchange efforts, hire graduates of programs that prepare students with linguistic and area skills, and engage in joint enterprises with educational institutions and their partners in other sectors. More needs to be done, however, to convince the corporate sector that it is in their interests, both long- and short-term, to become more fully engaged in efforts by universities and other educational enterprises to enhance exchange efforts between these two countries.

Further indications of the revival of local initiatives as opposed to national efforts can be seen among the higher education communities. Universities and colleges have increasingly been seeking ways to ally with counterparts in Japan for exchange purposes while seeking funding and support from a variety of sources. Sometimes these sources are in Japan but often are a mixture of local U.S. support (both private and public), support from Japan, and self-financing by students. This is a positive trend as it demonstrates the creativity with which colleges and universities are facing the declining national role. It needs to be encouraged and further studied. What appears certain is that the old model of bilateral relations, national-level large organization funding and leadership is being displaced by a melange of multilateral and locally based efforts. Examples of such local, multilateral ventures will be examined below.

Linking Across Generations

A perceptual problem exists in the United States regarding the career costs of participating in overseas exchange programs. Highly trained specialists in certain business and scientific fields are reluctant to go to Japan for fear of losing their position in their home organization or fear of losing a degree of professional "sharpness" if they are away from their field and institution. There are also problems related to the view that there is little to learn from Japan in certain fields. While this may have once been true, Japan now is a world leader in several scientific and professional fields. While it was once difficult for U.S. scientists and technicians to gain access to Japanese laboratories and other scientific enterprises, recent agreements between the two countries have provided not only easier access but also funding for U.S. exchange visitors. These changes notwithstanding, few Americans have taken advantage of these new opportunities. Another obstacle is the feeling that they will somehow "lose out" if they leave their home institutions. A better understanding of the advantages of such exchanges needs to be communicated to the scientific field, much as the CIBER programs have had an impact on the business sector.

Recent CIBER graduates can attest to the advantages they gained by being part of the various kinds of business exchanges, language training, and internships they received as CIBER students. Department of Education statistics show that such graduates were much sought after by personnel officers of major corporations.

Again, shifting the focus from bilateral to multilateral approaches should also help resolve this particular problem in the exchange relationship. Building linkages between universities, corporations, government agencies, and laboratories will provide a clearer and more accurate image of what happens to highly trained personnel who choose to engage in one of the many exchange opportunities available. Such knowledge should go a long way toward correcting the perceptual problem discussed above.

From Bilateral to Multilateral Linkages

It is now time to turn to some specific examples of shifting from bilateral to multilateral linkages. Several references above have praised such a shift, and it appears that it is taking place at a steady pace. There are important implications for universities, corporate organizations, government relations, and the previous structure of the U.S.-Japan exchange relationship. We will examine three categories of multilateral relations to provide a brief overview of how this has been working (and in some cases, not working) in practice: alternative higher educational initiatives, branch schools, and CIBER-type (business school exchange) programs.

One new initiative involving eight Asian nations and promoted by the Australian government is the UMAP program (University Mobility in Asia and the Pacific). The Australian government has provided funding to offer grants to support Australian universities in developing faculty and student exchanges throughout the Asian region. UMAP is an example of a large-scale multinational, two-way exchange program designed to encourage Australian students to experience one or more semesters in an Asian university, while allowing students and faculty from the participating Asian universities the opportunity to study in Australia. Fee waivers and full academic credit transfer are important features of this program. The program is open to all disciplines and is designed to facilitate mobility in the region. Developed essentially as a consortium, UMAP is intended to remove the typical barriers to exchanges (credit transfers, visa requirements, fees, etc.) by engaging in a number of bilateral agreements with participating nations. An assessment has not been carried out as to the effectiveness of this program, but it represents a trend toward mitigating the barriers to expanded exchange while recognizing the value of training for Transnational Competence. In 1995, 314 Australian students took part in the program, 63 of them going to Japan.

An earlier effort to develop in-country capacity to increase study abroad was the branch school movement in Japan. The development of branch schools in Japan is by now well-known, as is the rather rapid decline of this phenomenon. In spite of the many problems that have come to characterize branch campuses, several important lessons were learned and may serve to spur a rethinking of this interesting concept.

The branch school movement was a first effort at utilizing joint partnerships and innovative arrangements to increase the capacity for U.S. students to study in Japan and to bring U.S.-style education to Japanese undergraduates. Variations on this model could possibly result in a new joint-venture model, one that retained some of the innovative financial features, did not rely solely on transplanting U.S. institutions to Japan but rather formed true partnerships with Japanese institutions, and managed the programs in a more reciprocal, joint manner. Such an arrangement would solve many of the problems that plagued the early branch campus movement. Many of the supporters of U.S. branch campuses in Japan believed that the presence of such campuses would create a new flexibility in Japanese higher education and strengthen teaching and research techniques within Japanese colleges and universities. The very fact that they were outside the Japanese system, however, almost assured that this would not take place. A new model which links U.S. universities more closely with one or more Japanese counterparts would move much closer toward satisfying some of the initial enthusiasm Japanese supporters of branch schools had.

Some suggestions for how to improve on the branch school model include developing updated standards for the administration and operation of U.S. colleges and university programs in Japan while assuring that the quality of matching institutions is sufficient (faculty qualifications, admissions requirements, overall academic standards) and eventually developing standards of "equivalency" between institutions. The experience of Temple University, one of the most successful of the branch campus models, suggests that a critical factor is the successful recruitment and maintenance of faculty from the home campus. Those campuses that have survived in Japan are worthy of further study and efforts need to be made to develop new models based on the principles of joint United States, Japan, and corporate cooperation.

Specialized programs have also evolved in the past few years that auger well for new multilateral relations. Examples are beginning to appear across several professional disciplines, often at the graduate level, and focus on specialized degrees that require language, area, and internship experience and expertise. Again, these are often a mix of government, higher education, and corporate cooperation. One such example is a program that has developed as a result of the CIBER funding provided by the U.S. Department of Education.

These programs are funded jointly by U.S. government funds, the participating U.S. and Japanese counterpart universities, and corporate intern companies, who hire and pay salaries to the interns. The program is more costly, lasting about six months longer than an average M.B.A., but graduates have been highly prized by company recruiters, attesting to the demand and success of these programs in their initial stages. Such programs are not likely to dramatically increase the number of U.S. students studying in Japan, but they will provide valuable, specialized, demand-driven, and cost-effective programs of the multilateral variety that bring together the key actors necessary to increase study options for U.S. students.

Mobilizing the Grassroots.

There is a certain irony in the current U.S.-Japan educational exchange relationship. The nation that is typically thought of as inward-looking and provincial—Japan—is in fact the one sending the most students abroad, and the nation thought to be the most international, the United States, appears quite domestic when it comes to international exchanges, especially with Japan. Certain assumptions seem to be held in the United States that there is not much to learn from others, while in Japan, the assumption that real knowledge resides abroad may be overworked. Neither side seems comfortable with these new relations, and in fact, in Japan one sometimes hears educators remark in wonder why U.S. students would want to come to Japan in any case.

In the United States, however, almost the opposite can be said. Grassroots exchange programs are literally grassroots, with little or no governmental sustained support. Most often the efforts are staffed with volunteer support that comes and goes; what little government support that might exist is at the local (often city) level; and changes are made depending on current status of the local government. Funding is haphazard and unpredictable, sometimes drying up in the middle of a project. This lack of coordination and predictability is baffling to the Japanese and more than once has resulted in embarrassing situations for the U.S. side. This lack of fit between the nature of leadership and the structure of sponsorship is one reason for the slow movement of grassroots exchanges.

One intriguing possibility for not only increasing the effectiveness of existing grassroots exchanges as well as enhancing the potential for new initiatives, and at the same time solving to some degree the lack of coordination on the U.S. side, is to make more effective use of the network of consulates that exist in most major U.S. cities. Japanese consulates typically have an office for cultural and educational affairs and a brief survey of these offices reveals a willingness and strong desire to work closely with local communities in promoting grassroots exchanges. A closer working relationship with the consulates would also increase the coordination capacity as the consulates can communicate effectively with each other and through the embassy with the more centralized system in Japan, thus increasing the level of communication between the two systems and providing for better fit and placement of exchange opportunities.

Thus, in this new era of "thinking globally and acting locally," we should expect that local enterprises, state and local governments and other more grassroots organizations will become prime facilitators of future linkages and transactions. Just as many smart states are setting up trade offices in key foreign sites, so should they develop targeted strategies to nurture Transnational Competence. Several recommended strategies are outlined in Chapter Six.

Should Corporations Care?

A logical question at this point concerns the degree to which the corporate sector would be at all interested in the status of U.S.-Japan educational exchanges and the various outcomes that may emerge from a thriving relationship. What possible comparative advantage might derive from a more strategic involvement in a multilateral relationship of this type? Of course, both Japanese and U.S. corporations have long been involved—however peripherally—in the outcome, if not the process of exchanges.

In Japan, for example, many corporations have regularly required foreign experience, if not degrees, as a *sine qua non* for advancement in the company. This has meant in practice that Japanese students have persistently attended the best management schools in the U.S. To be a graduate of the Wharton or Anderson schools has been a plus for middle managers on their way up in the Japanese corporation. The same cannot be said, however, for their counterparts in the United States, where spending significant time out of the corporate structure, in a foreign management school, would only work against their careers. There is some evidence, however, that Japan's corporate willingness to send their best and brightest to the United States for further training is waning. Increasingly, institutions in the United States are being approached by Japanese venture entrepreneurs to set up U.S.-style management branches in Japan, thus allowing more Japanese executives and middle managers the opportunity to acquire a U.S. M.B.A. or equivalent degree without leaving Japanese soil. While this trend, if it is a trend, nullifies to some degree the value of going abroad for a degree, it still represents a desire for international training, learning the skills and methodologies of a profession as defined by another country. It will be interesting to see how far this trend moves along.

We have already noted the slim chance of U.S. corporations encouraging their staff to acquire foreign management degrees. What about the value of an international background (language and area skills attached to a professional degree, for example) in hiring and promoting personnel at the corporate level? There is mixed evidence on how corporate leaders view the value of internationality in their management ranks. A study by RAND concludes that in fact, U.S. corporate leaders value these additional international skills highly and seem somewhat at a loss as to why more such individuals are not hired. One suggestion is that this corporate policy has not filtered down to those in charge of personnel and hiring, who are still operating according to old assumptions about the preeminence of school rankings and discipline preparedness. They further believe that if international language and area skills are valuable for the company's foreign ventures, then it is cheaper and easier to hire locals from the country concerned (Law, Sally, etc.).

The recent success of the CIBER graduates in finding employment in top firms in the United States and abroad is some indication that this practice is changing, and in fact, some companies are indeed looking for and valuing M.B.A. graduates who also possess requisite linguistic and area skills. Whether this will also translate into an increased involvement in actively aligning with universities and governments in promoting increased U.S.-Japan exchanges remains an open question. There are various steps corporations could take to provide clearer signs of interest in U.S.-Japan international exchanges, listed in Chapter Six.

Generally speaking, Japanese corporations have been actively involved in enhancing the levels of U.S.-Japan educational linkages. This has been particularly true since the mid-1980s, when a sense of corporate responsibility began to emerge among those major Japanese corporations with large economic interests in the United States Corporations such as Toyota, Hitachi, Sony, and Mitsubishi developed funding programs, in some cases foundations, to support various aspects of the study of Japan, supporting both research about Japan in the United States (as well as conferences and other academic enterprises) and travel to Japan for U.S. students and faculty. Foundations have indeed played a major role in supporting innovative approaches to develop international education. We urge foundations to reexamine this area, as over the past decade the United States' performance has declined, even as popular interest in these opportunities seems to be on the increase. Several important activities could be supported by foundations that would serve to stimulate grassroots and state-level initiatives, as indicated in Chapter Six:

While the same level of interest and support among U.S. corporations and foundations has not been present, they too have become increasingly interested in certain aspects of the study of Japan and exchanges with Japan. These projects, and those of many U.S. nonprofits (like Rotary Club International), have provided a modest level of support for U.S.-Japan exchange relationships. But it is clear that if such exchanges are to move to a new level, both quantitatively and qualitatively, both the Japanese and U.S. corporate communities will need to develop new and improved approaches to the U.S.-Japan exchange environment. This would mean developing closer linkages with existing exchange programs, encouraging and responding to new initiatives for strategic alliances with U.S. and Japanese universities, and seeking ways to influence and link up with the variety of governmental initiatives already under way. Such a rethinking of the corporate role does not *necessarily* mean that corporations must increase their level of funding (although it is certainly needed), but rather that they be prepared to *respond* much more favorably than they have in the past to efforts by the other major players in the exchanges (universities, think tanks, community organizations, governmental agencies, etc.) to enhance existing and begin new exchange programs. This will require a new way of thinking for both Japanese and U.S. corporations—especially U.S. corporations.

A Role for Government?

Given what we have said about the declining role of governmental agencies in U.S.-Japan exchange relations and the need to move away from past undue reliance on government to carry the philosophical and financial burden of exchanges, what new, refined role can governments play? There is clearly still a major need for government involvement at all levels in helping to develop a new exchange relationship. The trend, at least in the U.S. government, to ask, "If this is so important, why doesn't the private sector do it?" oversimplifies the realities of past exchange efforts. In fact, the private sector *has* been "doing it" as we have shown by providing various levels of corporate support, private giving, foundation activities, grassroots efforts, and so on. The stimulus for this support, however, has been the fact that the efforts have been viewed as a priority by government, and therefore lending it a sort of legitimacy they might not otherwise have. Unless there is some degree of government involvement, leadership, funding, and support for U.S.-Japan exchanges, it is not likely that universities alone, or exchange organizations, can approach the private sector with requests for financial and nonfinancial support. They might well ask the same kind of question: "If this is so important, why isn't the government involved?"

The U.S. federal government has provided critical leadership in past efforts to strengthen international education, and we urge a renewal of that commitment as we rethink the U.S.-Japan educational exchange relationship. Chapter Six proposes five areas which are critical ones for government intervention.

Conclusion

In this chapter we have summarized the scope of repair and reform that must be undertaken in order to resolve the myriad problems that confront U.S.-Japan educational exchanges. Four main categories stand out: the need for improved *images and information*; the need for a reformed *infrastructure*; the need to address language and curricular shortcomings in the U.S. *high school*; and the need to modify and diversify the *collegiate and graduate programs* that are available both in Japan and the United States. There are overlapping areas to all of these themes. Improved information would help address the other three areas: infrastructure, high schools and colleges. And reforms in all four areas will be important for improving S&T exchanges. The issues that fall under each category can also be looked at separately. From language (translation and teaching reforms), to area studies (the search for diversified and alternative forms), to the branch school concept, infrastructure reforms that must be undertaken by the Japanese government, and precollegiate and collegiate reforms that must be undertaken by various communities in the United States, all are part of the range of problems that need to be addressed.

What seems clear is that the traditional approaches to these issues, which typically were focused on one particular sector or another (the government, the university, sometimes the private sector) are no longer as relevant as they once were. No one specific sector can or will take on the tasks that we have outlined above. There are some nascent signs that new models are emerging, however—models that reveal innovative strategic tripartite alliances between government (either central or local), the knowledge industry (universities, think tanks, pre-collegiate level, etc.) and the private sector (foundations but also private businesses). It is likely that if progress is to be made in a positive manner with U.S.-Japan educational exchanges, alliances such as these will play a major role.

Chapter Five

Getting to Know One's Neighbors

From the earliest days of Japan's commitment to modernization, the educational system has devoted impressive energy to understanding western culture and science, and impressive numbers of Japanese have traveled to the West for study and work. In recent years, as Japan has emerged as one of the strongest and most affluent nations of the late 20th century, these tendencies have been accelerated.

Japan's impressive commitment to understanding the West has not been complemented by a similar commitment to understanding nearby Asian societies nor the societies in other parts of the "South." Japan's international transactions increasingly focus on these non-Western areas and, looking to the future, Asia and southern transactions will rapidly expand. Taiwan and Korea have for decades been major recipients of Japanese investment. Today China is Japan's second-largest trading partner and Japan has more trade with East Asia than with all of the European Economic Community (ECC). Also Japan is a leading member of APEC and participates as a key player in other regional associations. And Japan's economic ties with many other southern nations are rapidly expanding. Yet the Japanese educational system still fails to prepare its citizens for this reality. There is little mention of Asia or other southern nations in the textbooks, and few Japanese students visit or study in Asia or other Southern areas. One can readily conclude that, just as the United States faces an "Asia gap," so does Japan.

So in this chapter, we explore various "improvements" that may enable Japanese international education to better provide Japanese young people with the competence to relate to their neighbors in nearby Asia and other southern areas. Among the components of Transnational Competence are the abilities to analyze new situations and to carry out effective negotiations with new counterparts. While Japanese education appears to equip its students with the ability to assemble and understand information, it may be less effective in enabling people to make effective use of this information. Especially as Japanese enter into negotiations in foreign settings, they find that they do much more listening than talking. Is this because of a lack of knowledge or poor language skills? Our Task Force concluded it may derive from some more fundamental characteristics of Japanese education: young people experience few opportunities to argue and negotiate with each other, much less with different people such as their teachers or young people from other cultural backgrounds because Japanese high school and college students encounter few young people from other cultures. Thus, in adult or transnational contexts, when they meet strangers, young Japanese are disposed to silence. The concern to develop a more articulate generation is a second theme in this chapter.

A third theme of this chapter will be to suggest improvements to make Japan more inviting for foreign students.

Just as the last chapter focused primarily on what will be required to improve international education for Americans, the focus here is on the needs of young Japanese. But many of the observations here apply equally to the United States. The American school curriculum has much to say about Europe and little about Asia, and American language education is similarly skewed. The focus on Japan below does not mean we think the problems discussed here are restricted to Japan; rather, they are the major weaknesses of a Japanese educational approach that is, in other respects, impressive.

Images of Asia and the South in the Japanese Media

Popular images play a key role in influencing the choices of young people about what they study and how they envision their future. Asia and the South are neglected in Japanese popular culture, which is primarily Japan-centered but also gives much attention to leading Western icons. Similarly, TV broadcasting features many Western serials such as *Bay Watch, Murder She Wrote*, and even *X Files*. But no Asian or southern serial comes to mind.

Fifteen years ago the same could be said for news coverage. The Japanese public is served by several national newspapers, two of which currently distribute more than 10 million copies daily. In comparison with the major U.S. newspapers, the leading Japanese dailies feature many more international stories. A typical paper has two out of its twelve (or more) pages devoted exclusively to world news, and international stories are also likely to appear on the front page, the entertainment section, and the sports section. Through the 1980s, international news primarily meant American news with additional attention to Western Europe. For example, our count of international stories in the *Asahi Shinbun* over the 1985-95 period indicated that 47 percent focused primarily on the United States and Canada, and 37 percent focused on Europe. The Eastern bloc countries of the Soviet Union and China received secondary attention, while other parts of Asia and the South were largely neglected. Thus it was something of an anomaly when, in the early 1970s, a crack Japanese photographer's pictures of atrocities in South Vietnam claimed space in these highly Western-oriented newspapers.

But especially since the early 1990s, this situation has changed. A review of international stories in the *Yomiuri Shinbun* over the Nov. 20-Dec. 15 period of 1996 indicates that the Asian region receives greater coverage than any other area: 38 percent of the stories were about Asia, compared with 16 percent about the United States and 10 percent about Western Europe; during this period, the war in Rwanda was raging, and partly for that reason 8 percent of the stories focused on Africa. Similarly, stimulated by the conflicts in Bosnia and Chechnya, 14 percent of the stories focused on Eastern Europe and Russia. A count of stories in the *Asahi Shinbun* from Jan. 12-Jan. 27 of 1997 indicated more stories on East Asia (78) than on North America (66), with Western Europe third (33) followed by Southeast Asia (24); stories about Eastern Europe and Russia were next with sparse coverage of other regions.

The remarkable shift in the Asian focus of Japanese news coverage may be followed by shifts in other sectors of Japanese society, but as we will illustrate in the sections to follow there are many challenges ahead.

Improving the Consistency of the Employers' Asia/South Strategies

A starting point for considering these challenges is to reflect on the vertical articulation of Japanese education with the employment sector. Young people in Japan look to education primarily as a means of obtaining employment, so the messages that employers send to youth and higher education about employer priorities have an enormously important influence. For much of the modern period, the employer-education links have been exceptionally tight in Japan, so much so that sociologists speak of a "degreeocracy." At least two elements are involved: the specific university attended and the type of degree awarded. Key employers restrict their managerial-level recruitment to graduates in specific fields from a small handful of higher educational institutions. For example, a majority of the senior-level officials in the national civil service have been recruited from the law and economics faculties of the University of Tokyo and Kyoto University. Several of the leading corporations restrict their recruitment to graduates of these national universities, along with graduates from certain top private universities. Similarly, shop-level recruitment focuses on graduates from a limited group of technical schools and high schools. Thus, the school a young Japanese attends is very important.

Within this pool of favored institutions, employers seek candidates with certain types of attributes. In earlier times, they might have sought individuals who had a reputation for good teamwork and loyalty. Noteworthy from the early 1990s was the interest, at least stated by employers, in such traits as global awareness, empathy with individuals from other cultures, and an ability to speak foreign languages. These new concerns, which are virtually the same components as those in Transnational Competence, were clearly articulated in a carefully prepared assessment of employment needs published by the All-Japan Federation of Employers (Nikkeiren) in 1995.

While the tight links of key employers with top universities persist, in recent years, due to stagnant economic growth and the growing competitiveness of the global economy, there has been a decline in the number of good jobs (secure and at the management-level) the top employers can offer. An increasing proportion of jobs consists either of opportunities in small and medium industry or term contracts with the top employers. The average waiting time for obtaining a job has increased, especially for young women and graduates of lesser institutions. So the hold of the "degreeocracy" is weakening. Still, this important message from Nikkeiren can be expected to have a major impact on the thinking of young people.

But the corporate message of interest in Transnational Competency will be far more convincing if it is accompanied by supporting behavior. The Japanese corporation is an inherently inward-looking organization. Boards of directors are typically composed exclusively of Japanese citizens, and in most boards the great majority have had long-term relations with the corporations they now direct. While many Japanese corporations now have extensive international networks, they still tend to be highly centralized with all major decisions at foreign subsidiaries subject to review by Japan headquarters. Partly for these reasons, the overseas subsidiaries of Japanese corporations are usually run by Japanese managers who rotate from the home base, and there are few opportunities in top management for foreign-born nationals. Moreover, the main criterion in appointing managers for these overseas subsidiaries is their understanding of home-base priorities; relatively little consideration is given to the Transnational Competence of the overseas assignees.

These generalizations on overseas Japanese subsidiaries are somewhat modified in settings where Japan has long experience and where foreign governments and communities exert counterpressure. Thus, it is not uncommon for Japanese subsidiaries in the United States to be formally managed by U.S. citizens who work closely with "consultants" from the home base.

And when the Japanese consultant returns home for periodic discussions, his American boss is likely to go along. Similarly, relative to Japanese corporate subsidiaries in Asia and Africa, a greater proportion of the employees of U.S.-based Japanese subsidiaries is likely to be non-Japanese. Indeed, even in the crucial area of research and development (R&D), Japanese corporations in the United States are relatively open. More than 50 Japanese corporations have significant R&D operations in the United States where they work closely with American researchers, sharing technology developed in Japan with the expectation that the American counterparts will propose useful modifications. In some cases, the U.S.-based operations are looked to for fundamental innovations (e.g., NEC expects this from its laboratory in Princeton, N.J.). Japanese corporations are relatively open with their technology in the United States because they expect this openness will lead to important advances.

To date, Japanese corporations have been slow to develop R&D laboratories in non-Western settings. There is not a single important corporate R&D laboratory in Africa and there are only a handful in Asia. Moreover, in these non-Western settings, Japanese managers appear to be more reluctant to include locals on their management teams. Thus, a recent report of the Japan Overseas Enterprises Association (1996) indicates that the percentage of expatriates in Japanese firms is 20 times higher than for European and American firms. In a related report, the Ministry of International Trade and Industry recently noted that Japanese overseas subsidiaries are not as profitable as their western competitors. The MITI report goes on to say that this may be because the Japanese firms are too Japanese and have failed to adapt themselves to local settings.

The failure of Japanese corporations to hire foreign nationals and to share technology leads to much resentment in overseas settings. This resentment can be aggravated by the cultural insensitivity of the alien managerial class. These feelings are particularly strong in Asia, in that so many young Asians have attended Japanese universities and obtained first and second degrees in relevant fields such as science, engineering, law, and economics. These young Asians feel they have the necessary qualifications and language skills to effectively serve a Japanese firm.

These observations lead to several proposals that deserve more serious consideration by the Japanese corporate world:

1. There is a need for Japanese corporations to give more attention in their recruitment of new staff to the Transnational Competence of the applicants. As noted earlier in this chapter, Nikkeiren in 1995 for the first time firmly expressed its support for this change.

It is hoped, as the Japanese economic environment improves, that there will be clearer signs of approval by the member corporations.

2. There is a need for Japanese corporations to allow their overseas subsidiaries to operate with greater autonomy.

3. There is a need for Japanese corporations to devote more effort to recruiting foreign nationals and to grooming the most able among these recruits for top management positions.

4. There will be a need for the Japanese government to reconsider its immigration and naturalization laws so as to make it easier for foreign nationals to work in Japan and/or with Japanese organizations.

Political Support for Internationalization

The Japanese Constitution gives considerable regulatory authority over education to the Japanese Ministry of Education and Culture (MOEC). For example, at the university level these regulations limit the establishment of new universities, faculties, and departments, and they even prescribe the number of students that can be enrolled in individual departments. At the school level, the Ministry-prepared Course of Study defines objectives for all courses, and this document is used to make rulings on the appropriateness of curricular innovations and even the content of specific textbooks. Through the mid-1980s the Ministry was very restrictive regarding many of the issues of interest to this report. However, from that time there have been two favorable developments. The first was the proposal by the Prime Minister's Council on Administrative Reform that Japan seek to decentralize and deregulate its governmental procedures. Secondly, concerning "internationalization," the Prime Minister's Council on Educational Reform (Rinkyoshin), possibly the most important educational committee convened since the Occupation, issued a report making this theme one of the top eight priorities for the future of Japanese education. In the Council's own words:

> To cope with this age of internationalization, we should upgrade the level of education and research at educational institutions, especially at universities, and make these institutions more open to the international community. Based on an entirely new mode of thought, we should endeavor to transform drastically our educational institutions from those which are operated exclusively for Japanese to those which will be more open to foreign nationals and which will be able to contribute to the development of human resources in the world, as well as to the development of science and culture in the world.

> Meanwhile, on the basis of the perception that a good Japanese citizen is also a good world citizen, we must establish an education aiming to provide students with a deep understanding of other

cultures and traditions overseas, in addition to an education aiming at fostering in students a love of our country and an understanding of the individuality of Japanese culture. (*Rinkyoshin*, 1985, p. 31)

Since then, there have been a number of promising changes:

The Japanese School Curriculum. The Ministry of Education sets various regulations that guide the direction of school education, including the Course of Study (a detailed outline of the curriculum) and a review process for the content of the textbooks proposed by various private publishing firms. This guidance has often been the target of criticism. For example, Ienaga Saburo, a leading historian, wrote a textbook on the Pacific War, and the Ministry indicated its displeasure with various passages, thus blocking the text's publication. Ienaga challenged the Ministry in the courts, and the subsequent legal struggle lasted for 12 years before the Ministry finally prevailed. While the particular way in which Professor Ienaga discussed Japanese colonialism and the war may have been objectionable, there still remains a strong sentiment, vocalized both by critics in Japan and her neighboring countries, that the available textbooks are not sufficiently balanced or detailed in their coverage of this period (*Asahi Shinbun*, June 30, 1993). This issue has become so explosive that former Prime Minister Maruyama's proposal for some public body to host a multinational committee for writing more balanced textbooks had no takers.

Rinkyoshin made several proposals for liberalizing school education, including the development of new six-year high schools, the increase in the number of electives at the secondary level, and a greater stress on active learning to foster creativity. Increased internationalization of the curricula and a greater emphasis on study abroad were also encouraged. Some local school systems have responded to Rinkyoshin's proposals, but overall there has not been much change in Japanese school education over the past 10 years. The educational experience is still highly regulated and parochial.

Recognizing the difficulty that young Japanese have in learning English, from the late 1980s the Ministry launched the JET program, which invites young college graduates from English-speaking countries to come to Japan for a year or more to help in high school and community English language education. Since that time many young foreigners (more than 5000 in 1996) have been deployed in Japanese high schools each year. This innovation has had a tremendous impact on the foreign visitors, many of whom decide on return to their country to take up Japan-related careers. And it has no doubt had some impact on the quality of Japanese high school education in the English language.

Distinct from the changes to stimulate the typical Japanese student are those to better accommodate the growing number of Japanese young people who accompany their parents on overseas business assignments and then attempt to return to Japan. A 1993 report from the Ministry of Education indicates that some 50,000 young school-aged Japanese were abroad, and nearly four-fifths were in local schools (MOEC, 1994, p. 54). The great majority of these children were in North America and Western Europe, but nearly 12,000 were in Asia. Japan's continuing involvement in world affairs will guarantee that many young Japanese obtain this international exposure.

When these young people return to Japan, they often encounter many obstacles. They may come back at an awkward time in the school year and be required to wait some time before being allowed entry into a school, and thus in some instances they may lose a full year. In other instances, they find that their written Japanese has declined so they do not perform as well as they are accustomed to doing. On the other hand, while many of these young people develop fluency in a foreign language, they discover on their return that their new ability is not appreciated by their peers (or even their teachers). Moreover, it is not uncommon for the returnees to find that their stay-home peers make fun of their "foreignness."

The returnee problem caught the imagination of MOEC reformers in the mid-1980s, and led to a number of new provisions, such as the development of special International Schools in Japan to receive the returnees as well as special repatriation courses at other schools. Also, some universities agreed to relax their admissions rules so as to exempt returnees with impressive overseas study experiences (for example, completion of the International Baccalaureate) from the standard entrance examinations. So for those children privileged enough to have parents assigned overseas, these provisions became powerful incentives to spend extended time overseas through the completion of high school (Goodman, 1990). But these changes had little impact on the educational experience of the much larger numbers of young Japanese who stayed at home.

Higher Education. At the tertiary level, internationalization may involve improving the curriculum of Japanese universities, encouraging more Japanese to go overseas, and attracting more foreign students to Japan. Concerning the curriculum, the initial response was the formation of a number of new departments, and even faculty, focusing on comparative culture and international relations. For example, among the leading national universities, the University of Tokyo has created a new study-abroad program and Nagoya University has established a new Faculty of Development Studies. In the private sector easily a dozen new international relations faculties were established. In the respective faculties were departments typically focusing on such areas as the international political system and law, international economics and development, and comparative culture.

Many of these comparative culture programs included some attention to Asia and other southern nations. But the programs faced difficulty in developing strong programs as Japan had few true specialists on Asia and the South, and the institutions were reluctant to recruit foreign nationals to their faculty. Partly for these reasons, the new programs tended not to offer much teaching of Asian and languages of the South.

Perhaps most critical is the weakness of these programs at the graduate level. There are possibly only five institutions in Japan that have even a half-dozen scholars with true expertise on Asia, and hence the ability to provide a broad-gauged training of Asian specialists. So most of Japan's contemporary Asian specialists have received their training outside of Japan. Of course, there are important exceptions: The University of Tokyo's Institute of Oriental Studies has many specialists on contemporary China and Kyoto University's Center of Southeast Asian Studies has more than a dozen full-time staff with outstanding qualifications for studying that region.

In the late 1980s, the government also eased its requirement on credit transfer, leading to an opening up of several new study-abroad and exchange programs. But as will be seen below, these have encountered many obstacles.

In reviewing the Japanese context, our focus has been on the large corporations and the central government as the major initiators of change; in contrast is the United States, where state governments, grassroots organizations, and autonomous university and educational associations have a more prominent role. Interestingly, in recent years the rhetoric of Japanese education is giving more recognition to these latter groups. Ever since the administrative reforms of the mid-1980s, the national government has acknowledged the need to empower local governments and encourage greater financial discretion at the local level. Also, about one-third of the 16th report of the Central Education Council (1996) focuses on local initiatives. In the future, local innovations may play a more prominent role in Japanese educational development.

Improving the Infrastructure

In the review of educational traditions, we noted Japan's determination to send promising young scholars overseas to learn Western science and technology. This export model of international education was not balanced by a complementary system for welcoming foreign students to Japan, and indeed compared to other advanced countries Japan has relatively few foreign students in her schools and universities. At the university level, foreign students made up less than 0.5 percent of the student body in 1980 compared with about three percent in the United States and over five percent in most West European nations. Concurrent with the Rinkyoshin Report, Prime Minister

Nakasone boldly proposed an opening of Japan's doors to foreign students so that at least 100,000 would be involved in higher education by the year 2000. Over the late eighties, the number of foreign students rapidly increased, but it apparently peaked in 1995 at 53,847 and actually declined in 1996. Given these circumstances, it is clear that the goal of 100,000 by the year 2000 will not be reached. Observers point to such factors as Japan's high cost of living and high tuition fees as important barriers. But those familiar with the practices in other advanced countries also stress Japan's lack of infrastructure for receiving foreign students.

Visas and Guarantors. Japan has a number of visa categories for foreign students, and most of these require extensive paperwork from the foreign student including a guarantor letter from someone in Japan. Of course, the typical foreign student knows no one in Japan, so it is difficult to obtain such a letter.

Among the visa-types are those for long-term foreign students who will pursue a degree at an accredited Japanese university and those for other students. The former are true student visas and allow the holder to apply for a rail pass, engage in part-time work, and otherwise conduct him or herself like an ordinary Japanese student. But the visas for most other categories of foreign students are more restrictive. Even students who seek to spend a year or more at well-recognized language schools in Japan find that they are awarded cultural activities visas (*bunka katsudo*) which have significant limitations. Over the past several years there has been much discussion of the visa problem leading to some improvements. But much remains to be done (OISO Kenkyukai, 1994).

Housing. Japanese universities usually do not prepare dormitories for their students, nor do they have international houses to welcome foreign students. Thus foreign students often find they have to seek housing off-campus. But in most locations, landlords express reluctance to rent to foreign students, and often ask for substantial deposits that are beyond the means of typical foreign students. Thus, foreign students may experience considerable difficulty in finding a suitable place to stay. Home-stays are an option, especially for short-term visitors to Japan.

Guidance. International Offices have tended to be modest operations on most Japanese campuses, oriented primarily to sending Japanese students abroad. These offices have often not been prepared for the rapid increase in foreign students brought about by the Nakasone proposal. Foreign students need assistance in everything from visa regulations to guidance in course selections and special counseling for stress and home-sickness. Even before the students arrive, they have many questions which they usually communicate in their native language. The international offices, often understaffed, experience considerable difficulty in responding to these queries.

Our examples of infrastructure problems are drawn from the university sector where, if anything, Japan's infrastructure is best developed. Several Fulbright supported programs are helping to train campus-based international exchange administrators. Turning to the school system or to local government offices in charge of sister city exchanges, many of these problems are magnified. Of course, Japan is not unique in the inadequacy of her infrastructure. However, in view of Japan's ambition to rapidly increase the influx of foreign visitors, these limitations stand out as issues requiring significant improvements.

Internationalizing School Education

The rules and regulations that shape Japanese schools currently place strong emphasis on the cultural integrity of Japan, and from that base provide young Japanese with tools to relate to the English-speaking West. The rules do not encourage relations with other parts of the world, nor do they allow major questioning of Japan's national identity. For young Japanese to develop Transnational Competence, a number of changes may be in order. Possibly, the most obvious and fundamental change is **the diversification of language education**. Currently English is stressed from the first year of the junior secondary level (current reforms will result in some English instruction from grade 4). At the senior secondary level, those students in the humanities track are expected to take up a second language. Official regulations do not specify the additional languages that should (or should not) be offered, but French and German are the languages given explicit attention in the official Course of Study. These, along with Chinese, are available in quite a few senior secondary schools, but the languages of other of Japan's neighboring countries (notably Russian, Vietnamese, Thai and Indonesian) are offered in relatively few schools.

There are a number of reasons why the Japanese schools limit the languages they offer:

1. University entrance examinations generally focus on English and the major European languages, so secondary schools doubt that students would be interested in other languages. **Japanese universities should broaden their entrance criteria to give greater recognition to young people who take the time to learn unusual languages**.

2. To teach new languages, the schools need to find, appoint, and pay teachers. Finding people who can speak these languages is no longer difficult, as there are many foreigners in Japan who might be willing to teach, and there are also an increasing number of

Japanese who have competence in these languages. But several factors are said to stand in the way of appointing these talented individuals as teachers:

a) No single school would have sufficient demand in a particular language to justify an appointment, so the teaching appointment would have to be district-wide, which is unusual for instructional positions (though it is common for school inspectors).

b) Few of the individuals talented in these new languages have teacher certification.

c) The MOEC has not indicated its willingness to assist in paying the salaries for such.

Clearly, diversification of language education will require some central leadership. Among the many possible options would be a decision to appoint teachers in selected languages at the district level either on a temporary or permanent basis. If the temporary option is chosen, **the MOEC might consider extending its JET program to nationals from Spanish-speaking and Chinese-speaking settings and young people who know other important languages**. Alternately, foreign students might be given special grants enabling them to study part-time at a university tuition-free while paying back their expenses through part-time language teaching.

A second major thrust in school education should be **to place more stress on the strengths of other cultures, especially in nearby Asia, and to explore the dynamics of multiculturalism.** Japanese schooling is little different from that of other countries in its strong emphasis on "fostering in students a love of our country and an understanding of the individuality of Japanese culture." Some commentators maintain that Japan needs to strengthen this latter emphasis, and the prominence of their views apparently acts as a brake on efforts to give a more international and multicultural slant to the curriculum.

Educators around the world are only beginning to explore the essentials of multicultural education, and the debates on the best approaches are often quite heated. But the necessity of such education at an early age is no longer questioned. The transnational age inevitably leads to frequent interaction with people from other countries, and such interaction is more successful if it is based on mutual respect. Multicultural education seeks to build mutual respect through emphasizing the human dignity of all, and the indisputable fact that there may be more than one perspective on events, both past and present.

Japan's social studies texts devote extensive attention to Japanese history and to Japan's relations with the West, but their treatment of Asia and the

South is truncated and largely focuses on the achievements of ancient civilizations. The Sino-Japanese and Russo-Japanese wars are treated essentially as necessary actions by Japan to gain parity with the western imperial powers, and Japan's harsh policies in its colonial territories as well as Japan's wartime activities are essentially bypassed. These shortcomings have received much critical attention in recent years. **An important first step in multicultural education would be to build better balance into textbook treatments of Japan's relations with Asia and the South over the modern period**.

While Japan's constitution declares a commitment to international peace, Japan's moral education curriculum focuses almost exclusively on relations among Japanese people. As the nature of Japan's daily interactions becomes increasingly internationalized, it makes sense for Japanese educators to consider a broadening of the moral education curriculum to include more international examples. The curriculum already includes short biographies of a number of exemplary foreign heroes such as Marie Curie, Abraham Lincoln, and Mahatma Gandhi, to mention a few. **A new thrust would be to include examples where Japanese nationals interact with people from other nations**. An important component of Transnational Competence is skill in negotiating with people from other nations, and this could become a subtheme. It is possible that a focus on international negotiating skills might even help Japanese young people to develop new perspectives for coping with the conflicts they encounter.

Internationalization is a constant theme of the reports of the Central Council on Education (Chukyoshin). The latest Chukyoshin report (July,1996) continues the internationalization theme, with a number of new proposals for broadening the cultural exposure of Japanese young people. For example, it urges the establishment of new six- year high schools (combining the junior and senior highs in a single physical and curricular entity), and allowing some of these new high schools to place significant stress on new foreign languages. The Council also suggests the development of special primary schools where much of the instruction is conducted exclusively in foreign languages.

Japan's increasing interaction with the world results in a large number of Japanese living overseas, and often the overseas parents place their children in local schools. But the young Japanese overseas are only a small minority of all Japanese young people, and they tend to have parents from the managerial classes who reside in Japan's major cities. There are many other Japanese young people who will lack the chance for overseas exposure unless special measures are taken. The expansion of sister city relations and the promotion of youth exchanges will help other young people to receive the same opportunities for exposure to new people and points of view. It is hoped that local governments and grassroots organizations will respond to this challenge.

Improving University Education

Japan's formal educational system used to offer young people few choices, either about study or life. At the secondary level, about one-quarter of all courses were "electives," yet in fact there were few choices, particularly concerning foreign languages and culture. Similarly, as young people moved into the tertiary level, they were expected to apply to a particular faculty of a university such as medicine or law, and if admitted to that faculty they faced considerable difficulty if they sought to shift to another field. In recent years, there has been some liberalization in the rules on high school electives and university specialization. But concerning international education, there remain many opportunities for improvement.

For example, Japanese universities only approve of their students going abroad for study if the student either a) attends a special overseas program devised by the Japanese institution, or b) goes to a university which has established an exchange relation with the Japanese institution. In either case, until the late 1980s the overseas experience was not likely to accrue credit toward graduation, and hence only added time and expense to the student's normal program of study. Few students bothered to participate in these programs, and instead took private trips over their summer vacation or immediately following graduation.

In the late 1980s, two new opportunities opened up. The first was the decision by the Ministry of Education to allow students enrolled in a Japanese institution to transfer up to 24 credits earned at a foreign institution, as long as their Japanese institution approved. While international educators welcomed this reform, attempts at several of the more established universities such as Waseda to allow credit for study-abroad were largely thwarted by the powerful faculties. The mind-set that only work done on-campus in Japan is worthy of credit is a significant obstacle to improving Japanese university education. This mind-set is so entrenched that most top Japanese universities do not even accept transfers from other Japanese institutions, not to speak of foreign institutions.

But with this new flexibility, several Japanese institutions have developed new relationships with foreign institutions for study-abroad programs. For example, Asia University developed such a relation with a network of universities in the state of Washington and began sending several scores of its students each year. Ritsumeikan University developed a link with the University of British Columbia, including the construction of a special residential facility on the UBC campus. In contrast, others such as Showa Women's College acquired special facilities overseas to run their own study-abroad programs, staffed exclusively with faculty and staff under direct contract to the Japanese institution. In the first two instances, the Japanese students received credit that had value both overseas and in Japan, while in the latter instance the overseas educational experience was formally a Japanese educational experience. However, common to all of these examples is control by the sending Japanese institution of the choices available to their students.

According to one report by the early 1990s nearly 50 percent of all Japanese four-year institutions had established at least one exchange relation with a foreign institution (Kitamura, 1991). The United States is the major locus of these relations, and one report indicates that as many as 500 such relations are now on the books between Japanese and American institutions of higher education. A 1991 survey reported that only 23 of the more than 600 Japanese institutions with four-year undergraduate programs had an exchange relationship with an Asian university (ALC, p. 65ff). Even among these 23, the Asia relation typically opened up an opportunity for one or two students, while the same institution would have far more opportunities in western countries. For example, Asia University reported exchange relations for seven students in Asia and 683 in the United States. International Christian University reported opportunities for eight in Asia compared to 48 in the United States and five in the United Kingdom. The only exception was Reitaku University, which had 77 opportunities in Taiwan and six in Thailand, compared with 50 in Germany, 40 in the United States and 8 in the United Kingdom. Kansai Gaikokugo Daigaku and Nanzan University, both of which have large study-abroad programs and extensive exchange linkages, do not report sending a single student to Asia (Tanaka, 1991). While Japanese institutions have negotiated many exchange relations with western institutions, they have relatively few such relations with institutions in neighboring Asia. Clearly, **one priority for the future should be to increase the exchange relations with Asian institutions,** as well as to explore other modes for sending Japanese students eastward.

Particularly noteworthy until recently has been the virtual absence at Japan's national universities of programs either to receive short-term study-abroad students or to send their own students abroad for short-term study. But in the early '90s, the MOEC established AIEJ scholarships to fund foreign students seeking short-term study abroad experiences in Japan, and several national universities decided to establish such programs with English as the principal language of instruction. One immediate effect of the new programs for foreign students at national universities has been to increase the number of students from Asia, studying together with Americans, Europeans, and Japanese. The next step is to find effective ways to encourage Japanese students to study elsewhere in Asia.

The expansion of exchange relations is an important expression of interest in internationalizing the higher educational experience for young Japanese, but as currently negotiated, these exchange relations do not add much. Typically, an exchange relation is based on parity with equal numbers of Japanese and overseas students participating. In many of the negotiated exchanges, either students from the overseas partner are not interested in going to Japan, or vice versa. Hence the exchange is only a piece of paper. Indeed, according to the MOEC's statistics, only about 1,000 Japanese students participate in these programs annually.

While the study-abroad and exchange programs of established Japanese universities serve only a small minority of all Japanese collegiate-age youth, it is clear that large numbers of Japanese young people are interested in a meaningful overseas experience. Many of these young people conclude that the university-managed opportunities are too restrictive, so they go on their own, directly applying to foreign institutions for unrestricted admission to their degree programs. In 1995, there were more than 30,000 Japanese young people studying in degree programs at American institutions of higher education (and another 13,000 taking non-degree English as a foreign language). The great majority of these young Japanese came to the United States on their own, rejecting the option of applying through a degree-granting institution in Japan. Many of these young people might have preferred to have some affiliation with an institution in their home country, but finally decided against that due to the clumsiness and restrictiveness of the Japanese regulations on study abroad. **Clearly, there is a need to liberalize the restrictions on study abroad** so that the option of maintaining an affiliation with a Japanese institution while going abroad for study becomes more popular.

Perhaps even more fundamental than the non-performance of exchange relations is the fact that Japanese universities are almost as bad as Japanese secondary schools in their neglect of Asian languages and culture. Without some facility in an Asian language, a Japanese young person will not be able to profit fully from an Asian overseas study experience. Many Japanese institutions include some material on Asia in their general education survey courses, but not many offer opportunities for specialized study in Asia. Fewer than 40 Japanese institutions provide courses in Chinese language and culture, fewer than 25 feature courses on Korean and Indian languages, and fewer than 15 have instruction in the major languages of Southeast Asia. And of those institutions that offer Asian language, an even smaller number allow a student to graduate with a degree in Asian studies. The important exceptions are the handful of top-class institutions that are exclusively specialized in foreign studies, such as Tokyo Gaikokugo Daigaku and Kansai Gaikokugo Daigaku and several of the internationally oriented private institutions. None of the major national universities offer specialized undergraduate curricula in any area of

Asian studies. **Japanese universities need to strengthen their curricular offerings relating to Asia and Asian languages.**

Improving the Quality of Area Studies

Most Japanese universities do not offer undergraduate specializations in Asian studies as, with notable exceptions, they lack sufficient academic depth in Asia. Asia was not the focus of Japan's modernization drive either before or after World War II; rather, Asia was a means to other goals, including achieving economic and political parity with the West. As Asia was merely a means, it did not deserve deep study. Certain Japanese intellectuals and scholars developed deep interests in certain aspects of Asian society or culture, but the great majority who expressed interest in Asia satisfied this interest with intermittent short trips, where they conducted targeted observations or developed special friendships with indigenous collaborators. These relatively shallow explorations of Asia were sufficient to enable these scholars to include Asian material in their lectures on comparative politics and culture or on such thematic issues as the global economy, international organizations, industrialization, women's movements, or whatever. But few gained sufficient expertise to claim Asia as the primary focus of their academic specialization, and in only a few instances did their host universities decide it necessary to develop an academic focus on Asia.

It can be argued that the Japanese approach to Asia is ahead of the times. Oriental Studies was an important focus in the 19th Century European academy, and Area Studies caught the imagination of the American research university in the 1950s. The Area Studies movement in the United States led to the proliferation of a great variety of Asia-oriented centers and the creation of a rapidly expanding academic community which found its identity in the Association of Asian Studies. But much of the early funding for this development came from the U.S. government and the major foundations who believed that a deeper knowledge of various areas, including Asia, would contribute to U.S. national security. As these supporters came to feel more "secure," their interest in area studies waned; in its stead, these supporters came to express increasing interest in "issues" such as global trade, environmental stress, international migration, drugs, and other such matters that cut across areas. Area studies specialists, narrowly but deeply trained in a particular area, as individuals have often experienced inadequacy when they have sought to respond to these comparative or transnational issues. And the geographical division of area study centers can place obstacles to the development of multiregional teams that might engage in a more comprehensive approach. Thus, in recent years, on several U.S. campuses the efficacy of the area studies approach has been questioned.

It is possible that Japan, with its shallower approach to area studies and its greater respect for the traditional disciplines, is in a better position to respond to the current wave of issues. But is that so? For a response to issues does require a minimum understanding of the political and cultural context that shapes those issues. The American academy, by virtue of 50 years of commitment to area studies, now has considerable command of that context. It is less clear that the Japanese academy has that depth.

One way of approaching this issue is to consider the type of academic work that Japan routinely conducts on Asia. A perusal of recent publications from Kyoto's Center of Southeast Asian Studies and Osaka's National Museum of Ethnology suggests a common bias toward fine-grained anthropology, with the Kyoto institute also supporting some economic and agricultural studies. The research reports avoid controversial issues such as the status of minority groups, environmental problems, or political issues. The institutes tend to be productive, but much of their work is in Japanese and is not widely cited outside of Japan. Except in a few fields such as sinology and cultural anthropology, the best known Japan-based Asia specialists are those who have received their training outside of Japan. Japan's domestically trained area specialists tend to be less productive and are failing to reproduce a new generation.

While these observations are focused on Asian and South studies, some say they apply equally to the quality of American studies in Japan. There is a sense among American academics that there are relatively few scholars in Japan who have a deep understanding of the United States.

Japan's deficit in scholars with a deep knowledge of other cultures presumably could be modified if Japanese universities were more receptive to appointing foreign scholars to their academic staffs, but recruitment usually is closed and in the case of national universities is effectively restricted to Japanese nationals. This should be changed (Hawkins and Tanaka, 1995: 16). A basic principle should be to expand searches so as to seek the best scholar in the field, regardless of nationality. This is the principle guiding the scholarly searches of all great universities; to this end, announcements of openings should be circulated in international venues. Secondly, the terms of employment offered by Japanese universities, especially the national institutions, need to be reviewed. Top scholars in most university systems expect to receive a "tenured" appointment so that they can enjoy the academic freedom to pursue important issues without fear of interruption. Japan's national universities effectively offer tenure to scholars of Japanese nationality, but most only offer "contracts" to their foreign-born recruits. There are understandable reasons for this practice relating to the peculiarities of Japanese law and politics. The problem is that it is inconsistent with international practice, and it should be changed. Other nations with national or public university systems are able to offer tenure to foreign-born professors. The Japanese government might consider convening a committee of highly reputable scholars to review this situation and propose a solution that accommodates the often-voiced concerns of foreign-born scholars for equality and respect. A solution to this problem would enhance the international stature of the Japanese university.

Improving Scholarly Exchange

A short-run approach to enriching Japanese school and collegiate transnational education would be to make better use of the already extensive system of scholarly and citizen exchanges. Most of the scholarly exchanges are managed by the MOEC, the Ministry of Foreign Affairs, and their affiliated agencies.

One of the MOEC's largest programs, known as Overseas Research Fellowships (*Zaigai Kenkyuin Seido*), sends about 1,000 Japanese scholars abroad annually based primarily on the principle of equal distribution between universities and seniority within. Within the framework of research grants, MOEC also funds many applications for both Japanese and foreign scholars to attend international meetings and symposia. A third vehicle is the grants for international cooperative research, which in 1994 enabled 5,500 Japanese researchers to go abroad for extended periods and 1,000 foreign scholars to visit Japan. Finally, affiliated to the MOEC is the Japan Society for the Promotion of Science which, in 1994, enabled 2,000 Japanese researchers to go abroad and 1,600 to visit Japan. For all of these programs, the Ministry relies heavily on applications from scholars and peer review. The Ministry has no systematic plan for these scholarly exchanges, other than to realize more or less equal treatment between the respective academic institutions. The Ministry's programs are sometimes said to favor scholars in the natural and biological sciences and to be biased toward senior scholars from the West. **The invitees have minimal instructional responsibilities, have only modest interaction with Japanese students, and thus make little contribution to enhancing the transnational perspectives of the students.**

The Ministry of Foreign Affairs is more proactive. A major vehicle for its promotion of exchanges is the mission-oriented Japan Foundation and within it, the Center for Global Partnership. The Japan Foundation sets up Japan chairs and other related programs overseas, aimed at introducing Japanese society and culture to overseas audiences, and it strives to recruit good scholars/ambassadors for these positions (though it often finds it impossible to get the candidates of first choice). The Japan Foundation has made an immensely important contribution to increasing international understanding of Japan, especially among non-experts. With the rapid expansion of Japan's

Overseas Development Assistance, the Japanese Agency for International Cooperation and Assistance (JAICA) also has come to promote some exchanges.

The Ministry of Foreign Affairs and its affiliated agencies are also selective in choosing who to invite to Japan. So, at least in the case of the Ministry of Foreign Affairs there is a certain purposefulness in their work. But the nature of this purposefulness is not clearly articulated. Observation of actual examples suggests that the strategy is somewhat conservative, involving the invitation of those scholars and intellectuals the MFA wishes to favorably impress. **For the sake of more honest and open exchanges, it would make sense for the Ministry of Foreign Affairs to develop a more issue-oriented strategy and to seek a broader cross-section of international guests.**

Conclusion

Greater and more sensitive attention to Asia and the South is critical for Japan's future. Within Japan much needs to be done, and the central government needs to take the lead. The Japanese government seems still to be fighting wars that were completed several decades ago. The school curriculum focuses on the West, and is virtually oblivious to the dynamics of other parts of the world. This has to change. Asian students and those from the South are welcome as students in Japan's universities but not as teachers. Similarly, the corporate world needs to face up to the fact that it is very much in Asia but not of Asia. Japan's corporations appoint few Asians or citizens of developing nations to management positions, nor are they recruiting many foreigners, even those educated in Japan, for the management track. And until recently, corporate recruiters have shown little interest in young Japanese applicants who have taken the trouble to study a non-Western language. So there is also much room for reform of corporate practice. While many of the necessary changes can be effected within Japan, a few require cooperation with actors in other settings. These will be noted in the next chapter.

While the primary focus of this chapter has been on Asia and the South, we do not mean by this to suggest that these are the only problems facing Japan as it seeks to foster Transnational Competence. Rather, these are the problems that seem to be the most crucial, yet are receiving the least attention. Japan has an Asia phobia that has been heightened by recent and persistent criticism from the region over such issues as textbooks, comfort women, pollution and environmental destruction, unfair trade practices, and on and on. The approaches that Japan devises to increase public understanding in Asia and the South need to be effective, credible and compatible with Japanese sentiment. That is a big challenge.

Chapter Six

Action Agenda: The Fostering of Transnational Competence Poses Special Challenges for Reformers

The following action agenda, drawing on the findings reported in Chapters Three to Five, seeks to recognize the complexity of fostering Transnational Competence (TNC) through identifying the types of initiatives best suited to each of a wide range of actors in the United States and Japan.

Whereas earlier programs were focused primarily on a particular outcome such as greater cultural awareness or expert knowledge of the politics of a particular country, TNC is **more comprehensive**.

TNC requires **more time** to nurture; the cultivation of TNC may begin in the early days of schooling but will continue throughout an individual's career or life or through the community or corporations.

In contrast with earlier international education programs that were conceived primarily to benefit nation-states, the beneficiaries of TNC are **more diverse**, including corporations, local communities, and individual citizens, in addition to the regions and nations where all of us live and work.

Recommendations for U.S. Actors

To make progress on these initiatives, **it will be important for different actors to make contributions in the areas of their comparative advantage so that all can benefit from improved Transnational Competence**. The following are our recommendations.

The federal government has provided critical leadership in past efforts to strengthen international education, and we urge the federal government to renew its commitment by:

Declaring unambiguous support for the Department of Education's Title VI program that supports scholarly development. At the same time, increasing stress should be placed on initiatives that strengthen Transnational Competence through undergraduate programs in such fields as business and engineering, as well as on programs that specialize in outreach to schools.

Evaluating the various federal programs in international education, with the goal of fortifying those that strengthen transitional competence and retiring those that serve to sustain outmoded interests. A special concern is for a renewed commitment to the American Cultural Centers overseas, which provide excellent support to foreign citizens interested in the United States and its educational and cultural opportunities. Also, strengthening those programs that provide translations of scientific and technical materials into English should be given high priority.

Adding Transnational Competence to the list of national goals for secondary school education alongside the worthy objectives of realizing world-class standards in math and science. Transnational Competence would include a national expectation of high standards in foreign languages and culture, geography, and international economics.

Continuing through the State Department and other vehicles to urge foreign governments to reduce barriers to international education, such as awkward visa requirements for students and researchers. At the same time, the State Department in cooperation with the Immigration and Naturalization Service of the Department of Justice should be encouraged to improve, rather than retreat from, its tradition of hospitable and efficient treatment of foreigners who seek permission to study and carry out research in the United States.

Establishing and/or strengthening binational language training and research centers in up to 10 foreign nations of critical interest to the United States. A model for these centers would be the Yokohama Inter-University Language Center, which should receive increased support from both the U.S. federal government and the Japanese government. At the same time, these centers should seek to diversify their funding sources.

Foundations have played a major but declining role in supporting innovative approaches to develop international education. We urge foundations to reexamine this area, as over the past decade the United States performance has declined even as popular interest in these opportunities seems to be on the increase. Several important activities could be supported by foundations to stimulate grassroots and state-level initiatives:

The sponsorship of summer workshops and other opportunities to enable teachers to develop basic skills in critical languages.

The establishment of a new program to support the translation of important materials from foreign languages into English.

The development and distribution of language and curricular materials in critical languages.

The sponsorship of initiatives that enhance the visibility of opportunities for obtaining Transnational Competence; these initiatives may include funding to enable current actors to obtain the services of marketing consultants as well as funding for the development of improved vehicles for coordinating the information relating to these opportunities.

The establishment of national standards for Transnational Competence with an emphasis on national tests in critical foreign languages and in such subjects as geography and international economics.

Direct support for sister city programs in areas of programmatic interest, as well as indirect support through special programs to improve the infrastructure and the training of the staff who manage these programs.

The economic benefit of international education will be the dominant theme of the future, but this theme must be reinforced by clear signs of support from the **corporate world**.

It is urged that corporate leaders stimulate discussion of the need for increasing the Transnational Competence of their personnel at major meetings of corporate heads, and issue declarations of interest and commitment.

In the majority of corporations surveyed in this study, there is a considerable gap between the views of CEOs who highly value Transnational Competence and personnel officers who give virtually no attention to TNC in recruiting new employees.

It is urged that corporations reevaluate their recruitment procedures and information with the aim of providing more positive signals to young employees about the value of Transnational Competence.

Corporations as public citizens can do much to encourage local grassroots initiatives in international education through participating in local world affairs councils, and through establishing and/or supporting international internships for young people.

Corporations are urged to work with local colleges and universities in developing new programs that combine technical and cross-cultural skills.

Particularly concerning Japan, a number of opportunities have opened up for corporations to place junior-level engineers and scientists in Japanese corporate and national laboratories; corporations are urged to give more consideration to these opportunities.

In the new global era, the maxim is "think globally and act locally." It is expected that **state and local governments** will become the prime facilitators of future transactions. Just as many smart states are setting up trade offices in key foreign sites, so should they develop targeted strategies to nurture Transnational Competence. The following are several essential first steps:

The challenge of developing Transnational Competence should be debated at the National Governors Conference.

Individual governors should review the standing of their state in the development of Transnational Competence, taking into account the report card prepared by this project, and develop strategies appropriate to their state. Among the specific actions states might consider are:

Taking advantage of the recently expanded opportunities for sending interested teachers to Japan to learn more about Japanese language and society.

Making use of selected low-cost options for launching Japanese programs in their schools, such as taking advantage of foreign students on their campuses to use as language teachers in the schools.

Establishing special summer camps in international studies.

Creating high-profile Governor's high schools specializing in international studies parallel to those established (in many states) in math and science.

State governments should consider enhancing the status and quality of sister city programs through providing matching funding for staff and in-kind support such as office space, telephones, and computers. A coordinating office for these programs might be located in the state office of tourism or of international trade.

Universities and colleges have provided much of the leadership for international studies over the past decades, even though their primary focus has been on their own educational and research activities. Universities and colleges are urged to expand past efforts along the following lines:

Organize nationally to better coordinate exchange relations. Currently the number of study-abroad opportunities far exceeds those who are placed, often because the interested student is on a campus where there are no open places while a nearby campus has several open opportunities. A lead university system or alternately a major organization with experience in international education could provide the appropriate coordination at cost.

With great spirit and political finesse, back the renewal of the Title VI in 1997, and build on that political success to institutionalize new initiatives in international education by various national and local actors.

Provide support to local school districts in critical languages so that the supply of high school students with college-level qualifications in Transnational Competence increases.

Set explicit and realistic targets for study abroad participation on campus. A recent report from Michigan State University proposes 100 percent participation; another from the Higher Education Committee of the State of New York proposes 25 percent for all SUNY campuses. The national average today is less than 2 percent.

Consider developing new initiatives in study abroad that involve trilateral or multilateral formats.

Reconsider study-abroad programs with the aim of liberalizing university rules so that certain required courses can be studied while abroad; similarly consider 5-year BAs/MAs that include a more extended and intense period abroad.

In the United States, **local school districts** provide the financial and administrative support for school-level programs to cultivate Transnational Competence. Major opportunities await those districts willing to show initiative. The following are our recommendations:

Plan new initiatives for strengthening Transnational Competence, drawing on support from nearby colleges and community organizations.

Restore a minimum two-year foreign language requirement as a condition for high school graduation.

Take advantage of opportunities to send teachers to Japan and other countries for short-term visits or summer workshops.

Build consortia with neighboring school districts to develop sustainable low-cost programs that cultivate Transnational Competence through shared specialists in foreign cultures and other joint efforts.

Community-based organizations are looked to for important contributions to international exchanges, but at least in the American case these organizations have been troubled by weak financial support and voluntary staffing. The following are several recommendations directed primarily at strengthening the performance of these organizations:

Consider new initiatives such as multinational exchanges based on a network of overseas linkages.

Seek to professionalize the staff responsible for international activities.

Devote more sustained effort to revenue generation for international activities.

Recommendations for Japanese Actors

This section primarily focuses on actions that actors in Japan can take to improve the Transnational Competence of Japanese citizens, with special reference to their relations with counterparts in Asia and the South. Included are actions that may make Japan a more hospitable place for students and youth from other countries. For as Japan becomes more diverse the opportunities for young Japanese to develop competence in dealing with people from other backgrounds can be expected to improve.

The **Ministry of Education, Science, and Culture** (MOEC), through its curricular and regulatory authority, has a pivotal role in shaping Japan's international education, especially in the public schools. MOEC leadership in the past has enabled Japan to prepare itself for interaction with the Western hemisphere, including considerable improvements in English language education. The greatest challenge in the years ahead will be to promote a sophisticated level of Transnational Competence towards Asia and the South. The following are several key areas for reform:

The MOEC should encourage a true diversification of school language education. Current regulations allow local school systems to offer a variety of foreign languages, but there is often little incentive and the costs are prohibitive. Special funding might be established and new approaches might be proposed, such as the pooling of resources between two or more districts to enable the offering of certain new languages such as Thai or Indonesian. Special stress should be placed on Chinese and Korean.

The MOEC should broaden the JET program to include nationals from Spanish-speaking, Chinese-speaking, and other linguistic settings.

School education should place more stress on the strengths of non-Western cultures, especially those in nearby Asia, and it should explore the dynamics of multiculturalism.

In moral education and social studies, more non-Western examples should be included, as well as more examples of Japanese nationals interacting with foreigners.

The MOEC should develop a strategic plan for scholarly exchange that includes a clearer recognition of Japan's need to develop TNC.

Japanese universities, as the pinnacle of the Japanese education system, have much influence over the decisions of local school boards and parents as they plan their studies. Also, the shape of the university curriculum has a direct impact on the knowledge and orientations of young people.

Japanese universities should broaden their entrance criteria to give greater recognition to young people who know unusual languages.

Japanese universities should strengthen their curricular offerings relating to Asia and Asian languages.

Japan's deficit in scholars with a deep knowledge of other cultures can be improved by hiring more foreign scholars.

Universities should increase their exchange relations with Asian institutions.

There is a need for universities to liberalize their regulations on study abroad so that more university students can combine study at an accredited Japanese institution with a transnational learning experience.

The Ministry of Foreign Affairs (MFA), by virtue of its extensive contacts in the Asian region, has the potential for giving the Japanese public a clearer understanding of Asian sentiments.

The MFA should develop a more issue-oriented strategy to guide its identification of the foreign intellectuals it invites to Japan.

The MFA should reconsider immigration and naturalization laws so as to make it easier for foreign nationals to work in Japan and/or with Japanese organizations.

Japanese corporations today carry out more business in Asia than any other part of the world, except North America. Corporate personnel and technological policies need to adjust to this reality.

Japanese corporations should give more attention when recruiting new staff to the Transnational Competence of applicants and especially their knowledge of Asia and Asian languages.

Japanese corporations should consider increasing the autonomy of overseas subsidiaries.

Japanese corporations should devote more attention to recruiting foreign staff and to grooming outstanding foreign recruits for top management jobs.

Local governments should expand their sister city relations to cities in non-Western settings.

Recommendations for Joint Action in Improving Exchanges

Our review of current issues in U.S.-Japan international education suggests there may be a number of areas where actors on one side lack the information or authority to implement satisfactory solutions. In other words, these areas require a bi-national or, in some instances, a truly transnational solution.

It is our expectation that new actors will emerge in the years ahead to address these challenges, such as new regional foundations; philanthropy from transnational corporations with a Pacific Rim focus in airlines, communications and the media; the regional offices of such global entities as Rotary International and the International Association of Universities; and such international agencies as UNESCO, the Asia Development Bank, APEC, and ASEAN.

High School and Collegiate Exchanges

Our current glimpse of these transnational challenges derives from ongoing exchanges negotiated between pairs of mutually agreeable institutions. While two institutions or communities may agree on an exchange, there often remain problems that their agreements fail to address:

The Japanese and American academic and budgetary calendars are different, and this leads to a variety of **timing issues** that require immediate attention.

The most obvious example is the Japanese announcement of funding for U.S. study-abroad students which comes in May, as the availability of funding is not guaranteed until after April 1, when Japanese government budgets are decided. But by that time, many interested American students have decided they can wait no longer and have made other commitments for their summer or fall activities.

American students are not available to come to Japan until June, whereas the Japanese academic calendar begins in April. Similarly, Japanese students are not available to come to the United States until February, after the completion of their academic year, while the second semester in most American schools and colleges begins in January. While a revision of budgetary and academic calendars is probably out of the question, other accommodations can be considered, such as the development of short courses.

While there is a superficial similarity in the credit systems of Japan and the United States, a more careful examination reveals that what happens in a high school or collegiate course in the two nations is significantly different. American courses tend to be more systematically organized, with more rigorous requirements for written work and examinations, while Japanese courses rely more on student initiative. The differences in the nature of courses often mean that, even where an exchange agreement exists, **the institutions of one country do not grant credit for the academic work pursued in the other**. As a result, students sometimes spend a year studying abroad on an exchange only to discover on their return that they have lost a year, academically speaking. A careful study of these differences by an appropriate bi-national or regional group would be desirable, especially if the study led to a set of mutually (to U.S. and Japanese audiences) acceptable guidelines for the design of courses appropriate for inclusion in study-abroad and exchange programs.

One of the major obstacles to U.S. students attending Japanese universities under exchange programs is that Japanese exchange agreements often include tuition waivers, but make no allowance for living arrangements. Obtaining a satisfactory student residence in Japan (especially for a short period) is difficult and the cost of living in Japan tends to be higher than in the United States.

Greater consideration needs to be given to **enhancing the economic equivalence of exchanges** so that they include both tuition and board.

BEYOND EXCHANGES

While exchanges are an important mechanism for promoting transnational learning, these limit the opportunities available to young people and thus may be a factor in suppressing the effective demand. In the future, it will be desirable to strengthen procedures that enable a freer flow of young people. Just as the boundaries between nations disappear, so should the boundaries between universities and school systems.

A major barrier to evasing these boundaries is **lack of credit transferability**. Currently, there is no system for a priori appraising the credit-transferability of courses, with the final judgment left to those institutions where the student seeks a degree. An unknown but apparently high percentage of such requests is denied. Systematic attention could be devoted to the issue of credit-transferability with the development of guidelines that gain the sanction of key college and university associations. The European Economic Community faced a similar challenge, and in the late 1980s decided as part of ERASMUS to accord equivalence to degrees in similar fields throughout the region.

Most **funding for study abroad is tied to student participation in an established exchange**. Youth who take the initiative to break out on their own and seek transnational learning experience that is not approved by conventional exchange agreements usually have to pay their own way. Such students gain benefits from their independent ways; they are able to make their own choices about what to study, and because they are on their own they usually have to combine work with study thus gaining a diversified understanding of their new settings. But at some point in their learning experiences, they may need a break. This is especially the case for those in graduate studies that face the requirement of carrying out a sustained piece of research. It would be desirable for these young people to have some place to support their special needs. They deserve a just reward for their adventurous spirit. It is their spirit that will build the future.

Recognizing the power of the Internet, a variety of initiatives has emerged to publicize study-abroad and exchange opportunities. But **the proliferation of information is sometimes contradictory and thus confusing to potential consumers**. There remains a great need for a bi-national body to devote substantial resources toward designing and publicizing (through multimedia, including advertisements in major magazines) an information system that is truly user-friendly. The system should include information on both opportunities and funding and how the two are related to each other. This system should be backed up by vehicles through which students can receive personal individualized assistance with their search for information.

Joint Universities and Multilateral Exchanges

The above initiatives will contribute to the expansion of U.S.-Japan exchanges, but of at least equal importance for the youth of both nations will be increased opportunities to gain exposure to other parts of Asia. Especially valuable will be those opportunities that enable young people from several countries to interact with each other, exploring the various dimensions of multiculturalism. A number of collaborative initiatives can be envisioned, which would work toward this end.

In the absence of formal efforts to promote transnational exchanges, it is already possible to find many young people who use current structures to realize transnational experiences. For example, many Japanese young people now attending U.S. universities use the U.S. study abroad programs to gain access to Europe, Latin America, and Africa; some Japanese students even go back to Japan on these programs. Similarly, American students might consider using Japanese study abroad programs to go to China or other Asian locations.

One promising modification of current arrangements is to **structure trilateral exchanges** with school systems in selected American, Japanese, and Asian locations; and at the tertiary level between university campuses in the three locations. Young people might rotate between the three sites, with, for example, Japanese young people going to the United States at the time young Americans go to China and young Chinese go to Japan.

Another option is to promote transnational dialogue through linking several locations with Internet connections and, as costs go down, through live interactive TV connections. These **virtual education options** can be developed both for curricular and extracurricular purposes. As with the above options, they will require the cooperation of actors in several locations, and in this instance would most likely be dependent on corporate funding.

Particularly for the realization of these changes, it would be desirable to form an **action-oriented consortium of leading Pacific Rim universities** that would carry out studies to identify potential areas for joint cooperation. This consortium might propose formulas for region-wide accreditation that are mutually acceptable, and it might draft some pilot projects for trilateral exchanges. Providing the consortium achieved some success in these areas, it might extend its hand to take up new ventures such as a virtual university and specialized training programs of region-wide interest.

An option that may require the fortune of one of Asia's greatest entrepreneurs is to revitalize the dream of **building a great Transnational university that both facilitates interaction between representatives from diverse settings in the Pacific Rim and also is located in the Pacific Rim**. George Soros's work in fostering the Central European University provides a model. It is, of course, possible that such universities as UC Berkeley and UCLA, where more than one-third of the student body is of Asian origin, approximate this dream; however, these universities are still essentially western in orientation. The Pacific Rim University would have the high aspiration of training future leaders who are transnationally competent. It would welcome students from throughout the region (most of whom would receive some financial aid), and it would require students to develop fluency in English and one other major language. It would focus a major proportion of every student's academic program on regional issues, seeking to equip students with both an understanding of these issues and a range of options for addressing them. The university's classrooms and dormitories would provide everyday challenges to foster Transnational Competence, and in addition students would be encouraged to engage in field trips and work/study internships.

Internships in Corporate and Civic Settings

While much progress has already been made in developing new school- and university-based approaches to foster Transnational Competence, **the true test of TNC comes through facing real-life challenges in corporate and government settings**. Over the past decade, a number of U.S. and Japanese corporations have established internships to provide young people with appropriate opportunities, but most of these are not well-publicized, and the number is far short of current demand. Access to internships can be improved through:

Creating a greater number of internships in the corporate sector, and extending the geographic scope to include corporations throughout the Pacific Rim area;

Developing parallel internships in the public sector, both in national and local governments and nongovernmental organizations;

Consolidating information about available opportunities in a regional clearing-house coordinated by an appropriate body such as UNESCO or the prospective Transnational University.

Conclusion

This chapter began by pointing out a number of issues that require bilateral cooperation. As our study progressed, it often turned out that educational leaders wished to go beyond bilateralism to explore new patterns of international education that would provide future generations with exposure to multiple cultural perspectives. These educators had found that the addition of a third or four perspective leads to fresh and often deeper reflection. Following that lead, the latter sections of this chapter explored new initiatives that liberalize educational and research interaction, enabling individuals from several Pacific Rim nations to gain opportunities for mutual interaction.

The core members of the policy review group are listed below with the titles of a set of policy papers they prepared as a background for this report. The papers and this report have been circulated to a wide range of international educators and policymakers with the aim of stimulating fresh debate on the development of international education.

Traditions of Educational Exchange in the United States and Japan

Akimasa Mitsuta, Obirin University

Peggy Blumenthal, Institute of International Education

Grassroots and Community Exchanges

Yoshiya Abe, Kokugakuin University

Roberta Wollons, Indiana University

High School Exchanges

Kazue Masuyama, SUNY-Buffalo

Collegiate Exchanges

Yoshiro Tanaka, Tamagawa University

John Hawkins, UCLA

Faculty and Intellectual Exchanges

Toru Umakoshi, Nagoya University

Philip Altbach, Boston College

Corporate Exchanges

Shigeru Nakayama, Kanagawa University

William K. Cummings, SUNY-Buffalo

References

Abe, Y, Cummings, W., and Tanaka, Y. (1991) *Higher Education in Japan: An Administrator's Reference to International Programs.* Tokyo: ALC Press.

Adams, T. and Kobayashi, N. (1969) *The World of Japanese Business.* Tokyo: Kodansha.

Altbach, P and Umakoshi, T. (1995) *The Knowledge Network in Japan-US Relations: Advanced Communications, Education, and Research.* Working Paper. SUNY Buffalo.

American Council on Education (1982) *Foreign Students and Institutional Policy.* Committee on Foreign Students and Institutional Policy. Washington, DC.

Arnove, R. (1980) *Philanthropy and Cultural Imperialism: The Foundations at Home and Abroad.* Boston, MA: G.K. Hall & Co.

Association of American Universities (1984) *Beyond Growth: The Next Stage in Language and Area Studies.* Research Team. Washington, DC.

Beamish, P. and Calof, L. (Fall, 1989) *International Business Education: A Corporate View.* Journal of International Business Studies.

Bennet, J., Passin, H. and McKnight, R. (1958) *In Search of Identity.* Minneapolis, MN: The University of Minnesota Press.

Besher, A. (1991). *The Pacific Rim Almanac.* New York, NY: Harper Collins.

Bikson, T. and Law, S. (1994). *Global Preparedness and Human Resources: College and Corporate Perspectives.* Rand.

Bloom, J. (1990) *Japan as a Scientific and Technological Superpower.* Department of Commerce. National Technical Information Service, MD: Technology International, Inc.

Burks, A. (Ed.). (1985) *The Modernizers.* Boulder, CO: Westview Press, Inc.

Burn, B. (1980) *Expanding the International Dimension of Higher Education.* San Francisco, CA: Jossey-Bass Publishers.

Cassell, William C., Chandler, A. (1989) *Obligation or Opportunity: Foreign Student Policy in Six Major Receiving Countries.* (IIE Research Report Number Eighteen) New York, NY: Institute of International Education.

Choi, H. (Fall, 1995) "Reverse Brain Drain: Who Gains or Loses?" *International Higher Education.* No.2. pp. 7-9.

Coleman, J. (1984) *Professional Training and Institution Building in the Third World: Two Rockefeller Foundation Experiences.* Comparative Education Review 28:180-202.

Commerce. (1992) *U.S. Industry Access to Japanese Science and Technology.* 1992.

Cummings, W. and Nakayama, S. (1995). *The Nature of Corporate and Technical Exchanges Between the US and Japan.* Working Paper. SUNY Buffalo.

Davis, T. (1996) *Open Doors 1994/1995: Report on International Educational Exchange.* New York, NY: Institute of International Education.

DeCoker, Tezuko and Nakano. *Japan-United States Undergraduate Exchange Project.* CULCON. Washington DC. 1992.

Desatnick, R. and Nennett, M. (1977) *Human Resource Management in the Multinational Company.* New York, NY: Nicols Publishing Company.

Ebuchi, K. (1989, December) *Foreign Students and Internationalization of Higher Education. Proceedings of OECD/Japan Seminar on Higher Education and the Flow of Foreign Students.* Research Institute for Higher Education. Hiroshima University. Japan.

European Commission. (1995). *Key/Core Competencies-Synthesis of Related Work Undertaken the Eurotecnet Program* (1990-1994).

Fifield M., et al. (1990, August/September) *Workers for the World: Occupational Programs in a Global Economy.* AACJC Journal. 15-18.

Finn, M. (1996). The Stay Rate of Foreign Doctoral Students in Science and Engineering. in Todd Davis, Ed. *Open Doors 1995/1996.* New York, NY: Institute of International Education.

Gersterner, L. (June 5, 1994) *Complacency in Education a Threat to U.S.* Buffalo, NY: The Buffalo News. F9.

Glazer, N. (Ed). (1987, May) "The Fulbright Experience and Academic Exchanges " *The Annals of the American Academy of Political and Social Science.* 491.

Goodman, R. (1990). *Japan's International Youth: The Emergence of a New Class of Schoolchildren.* Oxford: Clarendon Press.

Goodwin, C & Nacht, M. (1988) *Abroad and Beyond.* Cambridge, MA: Cambridge University Press.

Holloway, N. (1996, May 9). "Counter-Attack: Corporate America Enlarges its Role in Asia's Economic Boom." *Far Eastern Economic Review*. 40-42.

Homma, N. (1993) *Comprehensive Research on the Admission of American Undergraduates to Japanese Universities*. Mimeo.

Hawkins, J., Tanaka, Y., and Nishida, T. (1995) *Rethinking the U.S.-Japan Educational Exchange: The College Level*. Working Paper. CGSE. Graduate School of Education. SUNY Buffalo.

Ilon, L and Paulino, A. (1996) *U.S. Demand for International Training: A Comparative Market Analysis*. Working Paper. CGSE. Graduate School of Education. SUNY Buffalo.

IMF.(Annual) Direction of Trade Statistics Yearbook.

Japan-US. Cultural Committee (1992). *Japan-United States Academic Exchanges: Trends, Opportunities, and Barriers*. Washington, DC: CULCON

Johnson, C. (1995) *Japan: Who governs?* New York, NY: W.W. Norton & Company.

Kawakami, S. (1994, July 4). "Local Problems" *Far Eastern Economic Review*. 159(27): 44

Kanter, R. (1995). *World Class: Thriving Locally in the Global Economy*. New York, NY: Simon and Schuster.

Kitamura, et al., (1991, March) *Koto Kyoiku no Johoka to Kokusaika ni Kansuru Chukan Zenkoku Jittai Chosa Hokoku*. The National Center for Multimedia Education. Japan.

Kishi, N. and Russell. (1996). *Successful Gaijin in Japan: How Foreign Companies are Making it in Japan*. Linclonwood, Ill.: NTC Business Books.

Kobrin, S. (1984) *International Expertise in American Business*. (IIE Research Report Number Six). New York, NY: Graduate School of Business. New York University.

Kojima, K. *Japan and a New World Economic Order*. (1977) Tokyo, Japan: Charles Tuttle Co.

Koppel, B. (1996) *Paradise Lost or Misplaced? The US-Japan Exchange Relationship and the Declining Role of International Educational Exchange Policy in the US*. Unpublished Manuscript. Honolulu, Hawaii: University of Hawaii, East-West Center.

Korn/Ferry (1994). *CIBER MBA Program*. Los Angeles, CA: UCLA.

Lambert, R. et al. (1980) *Beyond Growth: the Next Stage in Language and Area Studies*.

Lawyer III, Edward E., Susan G. Coven, and Lei Change. (1993) Strategic Human Resource Management. in pH Mires (Ed.). *Building the Competitive Workhorse: Investing in Human Capital for Corporate Success.* pp.-59. New York: John Wily & Sons, Inc.

Masuyama, K. (1995). *Foreign Language Education at High School Level in the United States and Japan.* Working paper. SUNY Buffalo.

Micou, A. (1985). "Global Interdependence: An Exponential Need for Business to Develop International Expertise." In *The Training of, and U.S. Business' Needs for, International Specialists.* Conference Proceedings at University of Massuchessets-Amherst. April 10-12. Washington: National Council for Foreign Languages and International Studies.

Ministry of Education and Culture (MOEC) (1983) *Course of Study for Elementary Schools in Japan.* Tokyo: Ministry of Finance Printing Bureau.

MOEC (1983) *Course of Study for Lower Secondary Schools in Japan.* Tokyo: Ministry of Finance Printing Bureau.

MOEC (1983) *Course of Study for Upper Secondary Schools in Japan.* Tokyo: Ministry of Finance Printing Bureau.

Mitsuta, A. and Blumenthal, P.(1995) *"Traditions" of Educational Exchange: Japan and the United States.* Working Paper. SUNY Buffalo.

Myers, R. (1983) *Ford Foundation Support for Education Abroad of Third World Nationals.*

Nakayama, S. (1994) *Kodo Gijusu Shakai no Pasupekuteive.* Mimeo. 94-105.

National Council on Educational Reform (RINKYOSHIN). (1985). *First Report on Educational Reform.* Tokyo: Government of Japan.

National Science Foundation (1993) *Human Resources for Science and Technology: The Asian Region.* (Special Report NSF 93-303) Washington, DC.

New York State Task Force on International Education (1995) *Overcoming Barriers to Study Abroad: The Case of New York State.* (A Report of the New York State Task Force on International Education) Ithaca, NY: Cornell University.

Ohmae, K. (1995) in *The Evolving Global Economy: Making Sense of the New World Order.* Harvard Business Publishing.

Oiso Report (1994). *Toward More Effective US-Japan Exchanges: Challenges and Opportunities.* Tokyo, Japan: Oiso Kenkyukai.

Overseas Study Action Task Force (1995) *Report of the Michigan State University Overseas Study Action Task Force.* MI: Michigan State University.

Reich, R. (1991). *The Work of Nations: Preparing Ourselves for 21st Century Capitalism.* New York, NY: Alfred A. Knopf.

Rives, J.(1984) *The International Market for Higher Education: An Economic Analysis with Special Reference to the United States.* (Doctoral Dissertation, Duke University. 1971) University Microfilms International. 72-10-896.

Rosenzweig, R. and Trulington, B. (1982) International and Foreign Area Studies and Research. *The Research University and Their Patrons.* Chapter Six (pp. 109-127) Berkeley, CA: University of California Press.

Rubin, M. (1996, July 5) "Interns Abroad: Students are Going to Give Their Resumes a Foreign Touch" *The Chronicle of Higher Education.* A43.

Schwantes, R. (1955) *Japanese and Americans: A Century of Cultural Relations.* New York, NY: Harper & Brothers.

Science and Engineering Indicators - 1989. (1989) National Science Board. Washington, DC: US Government.

Science Indicators. (1982) *An Analysis of the State of U.S. Science, Engineering, and Technology.*

Seward, J. (1975). "Speaking the Japanese Business Language." *European Business.* 40-47.

STA (Science and Technology Agency).(1992) *White Papers.* (Annual, in Japanese).

The Conference Board. (1996). *Managing Expatriates' Return: A Research Report.* New York: the Conference Board, Inc.

The Japan Foundation (Ed.) (March, 1980) *In Search of Meaningful Cultural Exchange Southeast Asia and Japan.* Proceedings of the Second International Symposium on Cultural Exchange between Japan and Southeast Asian Countries. Tokyo. Japan Foundation.

Ushiogi, M. (1989, September 21). *Internationalization of University as a Type of University Reform.* Paper Presented at the University of Sheffield.

White, M. (1988) *The Japanese Overseas: Can They Go Home Again.* New York: Free Press.

Woolen, R. and Abe, Y. (1996) *US Community Based Exchanges, Pre-Collegiate Exchange.* Working paper. SUNY Buffalo.

World Bank. (1995). *Workers in an Integrating World: World Development Report 1995.* New York, NY: Oxford University Press.

Zikopoulos, M. and Barber, E. (1980) *The ITT International Fellowship Program: An Assessment After Ten Years.* (IIE Research Report Number Four) New York, NY. Institute of International Education. U.S.

Attendees at Task Force Workshops

The Task Force convened several workshops to share findings and seek the advice and comments of a variety of individuals interested in international education . The Report owes many insights to these stimulating discussions, and we would like here to thank all who participated. However, we do not mean to suggest that the individuals below or the organizations with which they are associated have approved the report. The Task Force claims full responsibility for the report and its recommendations.

Los Angeles, UCLA, Jan 4-6, 1995

Yoshiya	Abe	Kokugakuin University
Philip G.	Altbach	Boston College
Akiyoshi	Aoyama	Rotary International
Ronald	Aqua	US-Japan Foundation
Nandini	Chowdhury	State University of New York at Buffalo
William K.	Cummings	State University of New York at Buffalo
Todd	Davis	Institute of International Education
Barbara	Finklestein	University of Maryland
Yukio	Fujita	Aichi Gakuin University
Stanley	Heginbothan	New York Academy of Science
Kazuyuki	Kitamura	National Institute of Educational Research
Fumio	Kodama	University of Tokyo
Chuko	Koide	Aichi Gakuen Universitiy
Masahiro	Kuwahara	Aichi Gakuen University
Akimasa	Mitsuta	Obirin University
Shigeru	Nakayama	Kanagawa University
Donald	Nielsen	University of Minnesota/Akita University

Fred	Notehelfer	University of California, Los Angeles
Patricia	O'Neil Brown	Asia-Pacific Technology Program, US Department of Commerce
Yoshiaki	Obara	Tamagawa University
Kanji	Ono	University of California, Los Angeles
Philip J.	Palin	The Laurasian Institute
Samuel	Shepherd	US-Japan Educational Commission
Michiaki	Takaishi	Japan Society for the Promotion of Science
Yoshiro	Tanaka	Tamagawa University
Gary	Theisen	Institute of International Education
Toru	Umakoshi	Nagoya University
Roberta	Wollons	Indiana University Northwest
Richard J.	Wood	Yale University
Caroline	Yang	Member, J. William Fulbright Foreign Scholarships Board
Stan	Zehr	Rockwell International

Washington, USIA, September 15, 1995

Yoshiya	Abe	Kokugakuin University
Philip G.	Altbach	Boston College
Peggy	Blumenthal	Institute of International Education
William K.	Cummings	State University of New York at Buffalo
Todd	Davis	Institute of International Education
Pamela L.	Fields	Japan-US Friendship Commission
John	Hawkins	University of California, Los Angeles
Masamichi	Kono	Embassy of Japan
Kazue	Masuyama	State University of New York at Buffalo
Philip J.	Palin	The Laurasian Institute
Richard	Scarfo	US Department of Education
Brooks	Spector	United States Information Agency
Roberta	Wollons	Indiana University Northwest

Tokyo, Kokugakuin University, Oct. 13-14, 1995

Yoshiya	Abe	Kokugakuin University
Philip G.	Altbach	Boston College
Ikuo	Amano	University of Tokyo
Paul	Blackburn	US Embassy - Japan
Peggy	Blumenthal	Institute of International Education
Alan	Brender	Temple University - Japan
Anne	Callaghan	American Embassy
William K.	Cummings	State University of New York at Buffalo
Todd	Davis	Institute of International Education

Yukio	Fujita	Aichi Gakuin University
Barbara	Finklestein	University of Maryland
John	Hawkins	University of California, Los Angeles
Jerry	Inman	The Asia Foundation
Hiroshi	Kida	National Theatre Foundation
Kasuyuki	Kitamura	National Institute of Educational Research
Tatsuya	Komatsu	SIMUL
Julie	Lee	University of California, Los Angeles
Ellen	Mashiko	Waseda Universitiy
Mikiko	Mastumoto	US Embassy - Japan
Kazue	Masuyama	State University of New York at Buffalo
Manabu	Minami	City of Yokohama
Akimasa	Mitsuta	Obirin University
Tsuyoshi	Nakano	Soka University
Shigeru	Nakayama	Kanagawa University
Tina	Nishida	University of California, Los Angeles
Yoshiaki	Obara	Tamagawa University
Akira	Ogura	US - Japan Foundation
Kanji	Ono	University of California, Los Angeles
Hitoshi	Osaki	Japan Society for the Promotion of Science
Samuel	Shephard	US-Japan Educational Commission
Nakayama	Shigeru	Kanagawa University
Izo	Shimizu	Obirin University
Bradley	Smith	The Laurasian Institute
Yoritaka	Sugi	NHK
Takahiro	Suzuki	Sasakawa Peace Foundation
Yoshiro	Tanaka	Tamagawa University
Hiroki	Taura	Ministry of Education Science and Culture
Yasumasa	Tomoda	Osaka University
Toru	Umakoshi	Nagoya University
Larry	Weber	National Science Foundation / US Embassy
Roberta	Wollons	Indiana University Northwest
Shunsuke	Yamagishi	Asahi Shinbun
Shinichi	Yamamoto	Tsukuba University
Richard J.	Wood	Yale University
Caroline	Yang	Member, J. William Fulbright Foreign Scholarships Board

New York, IIE, June 28, 1996

Yoshiya	Abe	Kokugakuin University
Philip G.	Altbach	Boston College
Matsuo	Amemiya	Japan Foundation

David	Bachner	Hartwick College
Thomas A.	Barlett	State University of New York
Peggy	Blumenthal	Institute of International Education
Junichi	Chano	Center for Global Partnerships
Patt	Connors	BOCES - Erie
William K.	Cummings	State University of New York at Buffalo
Todd	Davis	Institute of International Education
Urbain J.	DeWinter	Cornell University
William	Farrell	American Chamber Commerce - Japan
Richard	Harrington	State University of New York at Buffalo
Carl A.	Herrin	American Council for Collab. in Edu & Lang St.
David	Horner	Michigan State University
Lynn	Ilon	State University of New York at Buffalo
Kazue	Masuyama	State University of New York at Buffalo
Akimasa	Mitsuta	Obirin University
Fred	Notehelfer	University of California, Los Angeles
Kanji	Ono	University of California, Los Angeles
Malcolm	Richardson	President's Commission for Arts and Humanities
Sherry	Ranes	Social Science Research Council
Gabriele	Strauch	University of Maryland
Philip J.	Palin	The Laurasian Institute
Barbara	Turlington	American Council on Education
Maki	Uchiyama	Japan Foundation
William	Vocke	Greater Cincinnatti Council on World Affairs
Roberta	Wollons	Indiana University Northwest
John	Wheeler	Japan Society
Kathleen	White	Governor's School - Pennsylvania
Richard J.	Wood	Yale University

Washington, IIE, September, 1996

David	Adams	Council for International Exchange of Scholars
David	Baker	Catholic Univerisity
Peggy	Blumenthal	Institute of International Education
William	Carroll	NAFSA: Association of International Ecucators
Robert	Chase	World Learning
William K.	Cummings	State University of New York at Buffalo
Pamela L.	Fields	Japan-US Friendship Commission
Barbara	Finklestein	University of Maryland
Virginia	Hammell	National. Association. of State Universities & Land Grant Colleges
John	Hawkins	University of California, Los Angeles
Carl A.	Herrin	American Council for Collaboration in Education & Language Study

Jean	Johnson	National Science Foundation
Michelle	Lampher	Youth for Understanding
Diane	Mailey	World Learning
Daniel	Maxwell	National Foreign Language Center
Michael	McCarry	Alliance for International Educational & Cultural Exchange
Margaret	Mihori	Japan - US Friendship Commission
Christine	Morfit	Council for International Exchange of Scholars
Cheryl	Ramp	Youth for Understanding
Lidice	Rivas	US Department of Education
Barbara	Turlington	American Council on Education
Roberta	Wollons	Indiana University Northwest

American Chamber of Commerce, Feb.1, 1996

William K.	Cummings	State University of New York at Buffalo
Charles E.	Duffy	Duffy & Associates
Robert	Neff	The American Chamber of Commerce in Japan
Kirk R.	Patterson	AIG Companies
Jeffrey L.	Plein	The American Chamber of Commerce in Japan
Brian T.	Taylor	Japan Health Summit Inc.

National Institute for Educational Research of Japan, Feb. 3, 1996

Yulia V.	Boyarchuk	Moscow Pedagogical State University
William K.	Cummings	State University of New York at Buffalo
Makoto	Haneda	Obirin University
John	Hawkins	University of California, Los Angeles
Akio	Hata	National Institute for Research Advancement
Kiyoko	Ishikawa	National Institute for Research Advancement
Kumiko	Iwasaki	National Institute for Educational Research
Michiko	Kainuma	Otowa Yurikago Kai
Tadashi	Kaneko	National Institute for Educational Research
Paul	Kitamura	Mandarin Oriental Hotel Group
Kazuyuki	Kitamura	National Institute for Educational Research
Masami	Maki	National Institute for Educational Research
Susumu	Makihara	NEC Corporation
Michiyo	Nagayama	Great Lakes College Assoc. Japan Study Program
Yo	Oshima	NEC Corporation
Takanori	Sakamoto	National Institute for Educational Research
Yukiko	Sawano	National Institute for Educational Research
Ryohei	Takahashi	Kyushu University
Hirofumi	Takemoto	National Institute for Educational Research
Chieko	Umino	Stanford University

Tokyo, Obirin University,   October, 1996

Yoshiya	Abe	Kokugakuin University
Akira	Ninomiya	Hiroshima University
Philip G.	Altbach	Boston College
Ikuo	Amano	University of Tokyo
Stephen	Anderson	International University of Japan
David	Bachner	Hartwick College
Bruce	Batten	Obirin University
Peggy	Blumenthal	Institute of International Education
Kenneth	Butler	Inter - University Center
Anne	Callaghan	American Embassy
Louise	Crane	US Embassy, Tokyo
William K.	Cummings	State University of New York at Buffalo
Jared	Dorn	Southern Illinois University
Stephen	Dunnett	State University of New York at Buffalo
Yukio	Fujita	Aichi Gakuin University
Glen	Fukushima	AT&T
Shuichi	Hara	ALC Press, Inc.
John	Hawkins	University of California, Los Angeles
Hiromasa	Hemmi	Association of International Education in Japan
Terumaro	Hiramoto	ALC Press
Manabu	Horie	Association of International Education in Japan
Jerry	Inman	The Asia Foundation
Masayuki	Inoe	Ministry of Education
Yashuo	Inoe	Obirin University
Masako	Ishii-Kuntz	University of California, Riverside
Izu	Shimizu	Obirin Gakuen
Hiroshi	Kida	National Theatre Foundation
Kasuyuki	Kitamura	National Institute of Educational Research
Kenjiro	Mukai	Catena Corporation
Hiroshi	Kida	National Theatre Foundation
Hiroshi	Magofuku	Keio University
Ellen	Mashiko	Waseda Universitiy
Michio	Katsumata	Nikei Shinbun
Manabu	Minami	City of Yokohama
Akimasa	Mitsuta	Obirin University
Chieko	Mizoue	Nagaoka University of Technology
Kenjiro	Mukai	Catena Bunsai Center
Shigeru	Nakayama	Kanagawa University
Akira	Ninomiya	Hiroshima University
Fred	Notehelfer	University of California, Los Angeles
Yoshiaki	Obara	Tamagawa University

Kanji	Ono	University of California, Los Angeles
Yasuaki	Ono	Ministry of Foreign Affairs
Robert	Orr	Nippon Motorola
Kenji	Sato	Asahi Shinbun
Toyoshi	Satow	Obirin University
Samuel	Shephard	The Japan - US Educational Commision
Izo	Shimizu	Obirin University
Bradley	Smith	The Laurasian Institute
Yoshiro	Tanaka	Tamagawa University
Akio	Terumasa	Exchange Japan
Hiroki	Taura	Ministry of Education Science and Culture
Toru	Umakoshi	Nagoya University
Richard J.	Wood	Yale University
Masachika	Yamazaki	Commission on Global Partnerships
Caroline	Yang	Member, J. William Fulbright Foreign Scholarships Board
Junko	Yano	Japan Foundation for Intercultural Exchange

IIE RESEARCH SERIES

Additional single copies of this IIE Research Report can be ordered directly from IIE if accompanied by a check for $10 ($8 plus $2 for shipping). Orders should be directed to:

IIE Books, P.O. Box 371, Annapolis Junction, MD 20701-0371

Readers of this report may be interested in earlier titles in the series. They are available through the Educational Resources Information Center (ERIC). ERIC identificaton (ED) numbers are provided to assist in ordering. Call, fax,or write to the following address for price and order information:

EDRS/CBIS Federal Inc.
7420 Fullerton Road, Suite 110
Springfield, VA 22153-2852
Tel:1-800-443-3742
Fax: 703-440-1408

Report 1
Absence of Decision:
Foreign Students in American Colleges and Universities
Craufurd D. Goodwin, Michael Nacht
(ED 232 492)

Report 2
Black Education in South Africa:
The Current Situation
David Smock

Report 3
A Survey of Policy Changes:
Foreign Students in Public Institutions of Higher Education
Elinor G. Barber
(ED 240 913)

Report 4
The ITT International Fellowship Program:
An Assessment After Ten Years
Marianthi Zikopoulos, Elinor G. Barber
(ED 245 635)

Report 5
Fondness and Frustration:
The Impact of American Higher Education on Foreign Students with
Special Reference to the Case of Brazil
Craufurd D. Goodwin, Michael Nacht
(ED 246 710)

Report 6
International Expertise in American Business:
How to Learn to Play with the Kids on the Street
Stephen J. Kobrin
(ED 262 675)

Report 7
Foreign Student Flows:
Their Significance for American Higher Education
Elinor G. Barber, Editor
(ED 262 676)

Report 8
A Survey of Policy Changes:
Foreign Students in Public Institutions of Higher Education 1983-1985
William McCann, Jr.
(ED 272 045)

Report 9
Decline and Renewal:
Causes and Cures of Decay Among Foreign-Trained Intellectuals and
Professionals in the Third World
Craufurd D. Goodwin, Michael Nacht
(ED 272 048)

Report 10
Choosing Schools From Afar:
The Selection of Colleges and Universities in the United States by Foreign
Students
Marianthi Zikopoulos, Elinor G. Barber
(ED 272 082)

Report 11
The Economics of Foreign Students
Stephen P. Dresch
(ED 311 835)

Report 12
The Foreign Student Factor:
Their Impact on American Higher Education
Lewis C. Somon, Betty J. Young
(ED 311 836)

Report 13
International Exchange Off-Campus:
Foreign Students and Local Communities
Mark Baldassare, Cheryl Katz
(ED 311 837)

Report 14
Mentors and Supervisors:
Doctoral Advising of Foreign and U.S. Graduate Students
Nathalie Friedman
(ED 295 541)

Report 15
Boon or Bane:
Foreign Graduate Students in U.S. Engineering Programs
Elinor G. Barber, Robert P. Morgan
(ED 295 542)

Report 16
U.S. Students Abroad:
Statistics on Study Abroad 1985/86
Marianthi Zikopoulos
(ED 295 559)

Report 17
Foreign Students in a Regional Economy:
A Method of Analysis and an Application
James R. Gale
(ED 331 404)

Report 18
Obligation or Opportunity:
Foreign Student Policy in Six Major Receiving Countries
Alice Chandler
(ED 312 981)

Report 19
Sponsorship and Leverage:
Sources of Support and Field of Study Decisions of Students from
Developing Countries
Alan P. Wagner, Elinor G. Barber, Joanne King, Douglas M. Windham
(ED 331 405)

Report 20
Profiting from Education:
Japan-United States International Educational Ventures in the 1980s
Gail S. Chambers, William K. Cummings
(ED 320 488)

Report 21
Choosing Futures:
U.S. and Foreign Student Views of Graduate Engineering Education
Elinor G. Barber, Robert P. Morgan, William P. Darby
(ED 325 026)

Report 22
Daring to be Different:
The Choice of Nonconventional Fields of Study by International Women
Students
Nelly P. Stromquist
(ED 332 633)

Roport 23
Priming the Pump:
The Making of Foreign Area Experts
Jackson Janes
(ED 343 497)

Report 24
International Investment in Human Capital:
Overseas Education for Development
Craufurd D. Goodwin, Editor

Report 25
As Others See Us:
A Comparison of Japanese and American Fulbrighters
Eugene S. Uyeki
(ED 365 205)

Report 26
Talking to Themselves:
The Search for Rights & Responsibilities of the Press
and the Mass Media in Four Latin American Nations
Craufurd D. Goodwin, Michael Nacht

Report 27
**Increasing Women's Participation in International Scholarship
Programs:**
An Analysis of Nine Case Studies
Rona Kluger